The Book of Rune Secrets

Tyriel

For Caitlin

Published by Rune Secrets in Vancouver, Canada.

ISBN 978-0-9877566-0-2

Table of Contents

I know I hung on that windswept tree,
Swung there for nine long nights,
Wounded by my own blade,
Dedicated to the High One,
Myself to myself:
Bound to the tree that none know
From what roots it rises to heaven.

None came with bread,
None came with drink.
Down to the deepest depths I peered
Until I spied the Runes.

Screaming I took them.
Recoiling, I fell.

Well-being I won and wisdom too.
I grew and took joy in my growth:
From a word to a word
I was led to a word,
From a deed to another deed.

Secret runes shall you seek,
Many symbols of might and power,
By the Great Singer painted,
By the High Powers fashioned,
Graved by the Utterers of gods.

Hávamál
(The Words of Odin the High One)

Introduction

Runes in the 21st Century

I am not a typical guru or teacher of the runes. Rather than try to convince you of my authority, I should like to impress upon you how lost the runes' secrets are, and how essential it is to believe in yourself and your own ability. No one has any final authority on the runes because the ancient traditions were eradicated. History is a master of covering its own tracks. This is a sad fact about much of our past -- one we must cope with as best we can.

In practice, authority on the runes now comes from an ongoing community of global practitioners, who have integrated these ancient symbols into their lives in astonishingly different ways. I greatly respect this diversity, and wish it could be more unified. But I am not overly interested in the "I'm right, you're wrong"-style arguments over the runes themselves. I am concerned with the concepts that the runes point towards, how we use them to signify, explore and discuss ideas important to ourselves and to one another. That exploration, whether individual or in collaboration, strengthens us and elevates us toward wisdom-filled lives.

When we cannot find the symbols to express ourselves in our day to day language, we must look elsewhere. The runes can act as a framework with which we deeply discuss important human issues. Whatever the runes were, and whatever they have become, we can use them as tools to contemplate and communicate fundamental spiritual and psychological experiences.

With the runes, we seek to gain insight and bring wisdom into our lives. We want more power to shape our destiny. We seek more beauty in our world. So you see, there are many things that unite us -- and when we reach that united mindset, there really isn't much to argue about anymore. We are contemplating and sharing -- all equally dumbfounded by the awesome universe we find ourselves living within.

How do we Interpret the runes?

The answer is: Don't be overly focused on the rune itself -- it is what the symbol points to in our lives that needs the most attention. The majority of the confusion I see emerges from a purely conceptual analysis of the symbol and its associations. This results in esoteric language that limits discussion and encourages debate over details. In Zen Buddhism, they call this 'a finger pointing at the moon', because it is like analyzing the finger when the moon is the subject. Each rune is a finger, pointing to a principle, a law, a force, or an energy in the universe.

The runes are an early form of western psychology concerned with introspection, contemplation and meditation. They can be used as an oracle, like the Tarot or I-Ching, or further developed into alchemy. They present a system by which we can organize our innermost thoughts in order to become more powerful individuals. The process of individuation or self-actualization -- of 'becoming' -- is beautifully enhanced by the study of rune meanings, because through the runes we study ourselves. From all this emerges the tangible feeling of magic.

Although many have wondered in amazement at the divinatory aspects of the runes there are much more powerful approaches. One of those practices is a form of alchemy, that I have used myself for many years. It was powerful enough to reorganize the structure of my mind to cope with the devastating consequences of several traumatic incidences. I have emerged stronger than ever, and the runes are integral to all of that.

Divination is something that may have got you interested in the runes to begin with, but there is a great deal of popular literature on the subject, so I will not be focusing on divination. Instead, I will focus on alchemy. Alchemy is the process of understanding both the positive and negative aspects of each rune, and transmuting our unconscious weaknesses and unrealized powers into conscious and enlightened states.

Along with this shift I will guide you on an advanced journey through each rune meaning. This by no means suggests you should quit your current practices, but this book will, if successful, lead you to more powerful and fulfilling method, customized to your needs.

The reason we try to tell the future with the runes is because we sense intuitively that the runes have something to do with the future. I will demonstrate that the runes contain a prophecy of individual and collective enlightenment, and can even tell us the story of how to bring it about. If all goes well, you can stop guessing at your future, take it into your hands and shape it however you wish.

You will notice there will be no 'mundane' interpretations in this volume, and nothing that will directly help you in divination as you may be used to thinking of it. However, you will benefit tremendously as I discuss how the runes might be used to understand and tap into the energy and principles of the world in a direct way. The purpose of each of these rune meanings is to guide you on a profound journey into yourself and your universe.

I try to delve into the fundamental essence of each rune, rather than present a loose and disconnected set of keywords and associations. I want to reveal the core energy that radiates outward into all its aspects, psychological, spiritual, magical and mundane. I want to show clearly how each rune differs from all other runes. Each rune connects to the totality of the other runes, and yet represents a distinct principle, power or energy. Together, the runes reveal a map of the cosmic laws, a formula of the metaphysical.

I was brought up by scholars, and I have a deep respect for academic research. Archaeology, anthropology and history are profound subjects, and many have taken this approach to the runes. We must continually bear in mind that the responsible archaeologist will insist that there is virtually nothing that remains of the culture that used the Elder Futhark runes. When it comes down to it, we can only imagine and contemplate -- and that is precisely what I want to help you do. But we do have the science of today to help us recreate our rune system. Psychology, sociology, ecology, evolutionary biology, memetics, semiotics, western and eastern philosophy -- all of this can be drawn upon. The runes talk about the same phenomena, with their idiosyncratic metaphors, that all other pursuits of knowledge and wisdom are interested in -- using different symbols and different methods, but all pointed toward the same universal truths.

Our intuition has been telling us that these enigmatic rune symbols can be used to uncover hidden factors and unknown rules governing our fate. They seem to let us peer into our present situation and sometimes help us glimpse the future, allowing us, perhaps, to take it into our own hands.

This is not an illusion. But it goes deeper -- the runes are used in a very powerful technique, a form of alchemy, a way of using symbols and concepts to reconfigure our minds so that we can bring truth and magic fully into the center of our day to day lives. Alchemy is just that -- transmuting the raw material of the unconscious into the brilliant gold of consciousness. With alchemy we transmute the mundane into the sacred, and free ourselves from the day to day habits that fetter our lives and impede us from living the fullest life possible. We can descend to our darkest, murkiest depths and rekindle the fires that make us shine.

Just as mathematicians and physicists use symbols to represent laws, principles and energies, the runes represent such things in the psycho-spiritual or metaphysical domain. We may not consider what we're doing a hard science, but we still want to observe correctly and produce results. Therefore, we are primarily interested in identifying real phenomena. Each rune points, through its metaphors, to something real in our existence.

Why Study the Runes?

Study of the runes is a study of personal understanding and power over one's destiny. Many people today try to 'see' the future using the runes. My system will teach you to see the present, and shape your future.

The runes are an organized system of symbols with deep meaning, and as such are gateways to examining meanings and thoughts about the universe and ourselves we would not normally be exposed to.

Understanding and living within the present moment takes much more than sitting in quiet meditation. The runes provide a contemplative framework for seeing and harnessing currents in your surroundings in order to take control and shape your future. We can connect with others who share our interest in these issues and form bonds and relationships that normal language doesn't always facilitate. Most importantly, we can use the symbols when we are alone, to organize and connect thoughts that hover only as whispers on the brink of our consciousness.

Truth, love, honor, sacrifice, courage, freedom, power, health, wealth, wisdom, joy -- these are some of the most important ideas to understand and live your life by. The study of the runes is actually a study of our 'most important ideas', why they are important, and how to shape our future by living in harmony with cosmic laws.

In figuring out how to use these tools today, we reach an understanding of how they may have once been used. A useful system of the runes needs to acknowledge that the Elder Futhark was never a complete spiritual framework -- it still needs work. That is our attraction to it, and why it brings us together; we can decide how to use the symbols, how to configure the meanings and what they mean to us. There should be no shame in that, and any authority who makes you feel that way should be held suspect. The runes are still a living language: a language still in use, still evolving.

Very little is known about the origins of the runes themselves, or how they were used, and for what purpose. That doesn't mean a lot of authors and researchers haven't spent huge amounts of energy theorizing -- they have! From scholars to popular new age best-sellers. You will have to determine for yourself which modern sources to draw upon as you develop your own understanding and your own system. I will try to provide some resources and ideas, but until you take your destiny into your own hands, no one else's system will address your needs in their entirety.

What we need to do is create our own process and guidelines, much like we create our own set of runes to begin with. I believe the practice of creating your own set of runes from wood, or stone or bone is a symbolic act that prepares us for the deeper acts of fashioning our own rune system. It is that act of transmutation that will shape our life, our world and our fate, and produce results. Real magic.

I have outlined the meanings of the runes, as I have come to understand them. I will then suggest a method for you to develop your own system. You may find many of the things I say useful, and you're free to use them in any way you like. I am honored and humbled that you have chosen to study my system -- I hope to someday study yours.

My practice is based on the study of the runes themselves. To contemplate the runes, to learn their meanings, to see what things the runes point to in yourself and in the world beyond -- this is already the practice.

This is a secular study of the runes. You may keep your beliefs, whether they be pagan, heathen, wiccan, asatru, or completely atheist. You may practice your rituals, whatever they might be. These aspects are not important to my system of understanding the runes. You can be a solitary practitioner and you need not worship any gods, or you may worship many gods.

My system is simple. It is not dressed up. It is not art, or science, or religion. If you want to call it spiritual, or if you want to treat the runes simply as shapes that have arbitrary meanings, like any other symbol, that is up to you. It does not change anything.

The fact is these symbols have commonly agreed upon contemporary meanings, which are worth discussing and contemplating. A focused exploration of these meanings is meant to improve every aspect of your life.

I wanted to create a book which was concise enough and portable enough that you could bring it with you wherever you go. It contains the most relevant and practical core ideas surrounding each rune, ones that should be considered best to always keep in mind. By no means are these explorations exhaustive or complete. For that, you will have to continue your studies -- there is a lot that has been written. But these meanings are empowering because they deal with energies, principles and laws.

In my system, I present a form of alchemy in which you discover a set of three runes which most fully represent your individual energy pattern. This rune-matrix is infused with a focused individuality to help you know yourself and navigate your spiritual and psychological landscape. As you read, keep track of which symbols draw you in the most and define you, which inspire you and fixate you. Discover three runes that you could solidly sit in the center of. This triad will become useful, and I will explain it in Appendix A: Rune Alchemy.

Alchemy will also help you with the comprehension of bind-runes, that is the combination of runes to study or tap into more complex or subtle principles and energies. Eventually, you will be able to form a matrix of all twenty-four rune symbols that represents you and your relationship to the universe, a snapshot in time. By altering the positions of the runes within the matrix and considering each movement and relationship, you will unlock enigmatic mysteries that have been unknown to you, but need not remain so.

There will undoubtably be a lot of questions left in your mind, even after extensive study of this book. Have faith that you can find your answers if you truly value the truth. I don't know everything about my own life, much less about yours. You can be confident that this is true of everyone, even the most respected of authorities. But I'll offer you what I have learned and I hope that you can improve upon it and pass it on.

What is magic?

Arthur C. Clarke wrote: "Any sufficiently advanced technology is indistinguishable from magic." I often see the runes as an ancient, but advanced technology. When I put myself in the mindset of those experiencing written symbols for the first time, it is easy for me to honestly tell you that the runes are magical.

But magic is what people call something when they do not understand it. Science often dismisses magic as superstition. We are so desperate for answers, that we often make them up.

Who practices 'magic'? People who seek the unknown. And who practices science? People who seek the unknown. It seems we can find common ground after all.

The world is a complicated place and our minds are question-asking powerhouses. We become interested in magic and science for the same reasons: we want answers, and we want power to improve ourselves and our circumstances.

We trust the truth, we seek the truth; without a true path energy is wasted.

There are very good methods for finding out the truth and bringing it into our lives. You have chosen to study the runes, and that is a good starting point. But do not limit yourself into trying to define what is magic and what is not. Either everything is magic, or nothing is. In either case, it does not matter. The universe is probably more amazing than we are capable of imagining.

The point I'm trying to make is that you begin your search for truth somewhere, and you follow it to the end. Be aware that the truth is a harsh friend; so are the runes.

In my system, it is okay to admit that we do not know. And it is okay to be skeptical. To ask new and difficult questions of yourself and others is the heart of enlightenment. My ultimate aim is to assist you in contemplating some ideas whose importance we can all agree on. By making these ideas central, your life has the potential to unfold dramatically toward its highest potential.

There are no teachers here. There is no ritual except study. Only the depth of your own contemplation will determine your level of mastery. There is no requirement for belief except to believe in yourself.

I will bring you as close to magic as I can, and the rest is up to you!

Basic Rules of the Elder Futhark

There are a few basic rules or features of the Elder Futhark runes, which are intentional and important. They may or may not be useful to you, but they are very important to follow if you wish to understand a lot of the work on the runes.

The order of eight symbols across, three symbols down is called the Aetts (Eights). Each Aett has a particular order that you need to be aware of. The Aetts are necessary to reconstruct the deeper meaning of the runes, and discover hidden relationships between them. Respect the order of the Aetts at all times, and you will decode a tremendous amount, more than any author could ever offer you. The Aetts may be one of the main reasons the system survived.

The position each rune appears within the Aetts should be memorized. Representing this order in a circle can also be useful, but remember that the ordered matrix of the Aetts is the most important structural element of the entire system.

The Aetts each have a progressive narrative, and so as a whole, each row is concerned with a different level of existence. There is also a kind of symmetry at work in their meanings. The first Aett has to do with our human concerns within the context of society. The second Aett represents our human relationship with universal principles inimical to our human situation. The third Aett represents the evolutionary cosmic law, from which creation emerges. I will go into that in depth further into the book along with the rune meanings themselves.

Each Aett also progresses from left to right, in a narrative that can be seen to transcend and include the previous rune. I have tried to make this narrative clear because it also teaches us how to see relationships between runes in a less linear way, once we are more familiar with the entire system. The rune columns are the best place to begin once you become curious about previously unexplored relationships. The first runes of each Aett, for instance, Fehu, Hagalaz and Tiwaz, have a relationship to one another as they represent initial conditions that are built upon as the Aetts progress. The last runes of each Aett are also concerned with going beyond the self, whether toward the community, our higher self, or our future legacy.

You will find a picture of the Aetts on the back cover of this book.

Advice on Rune Practice

While studying the runes, keep in mind that a rune meaning must make sense. How many times have we felt disempowered when something didn't make sense? An individual rune builds power with us as it becomes deeply integrated, understood and useful. If something doesn't fit our system, we must shelve it until it does, if it ever does. Concentrate on logical, orderly connections to build powerful results. We have enough confusion and disorder in our minds -- I'm not going to encourage the creation of more!

Another piece of advice. Some people use a blank rune, but I am convinced that this is a mistake due to the practice of providing a blank rune in commercial sets as a 'spare' if one is damaged or lost. Take your blank rune, if you have one, and set it aside. For all practical purposes, the rune Perthro, as I will later show, is essentially the same as the blank rune, so it makes no sense to have two runes in your set that would fulfill the same function. It stacks the odds in favor of the "unknowable" essence of the Perthro rune -- quite counterproductive if you're after knowledge of some sort.

I also wish to mention murk-staves, that is the reverse meanings, which are the perversions of rune energy. Past authors have often been afraid to do this, or else suffered from an overly positivistic outlook -- understandable, maybe even useful, but inevitably leaving a void -- what about the dark side? We know it's out there, and most of us realize we have one ourselves. Thus, a second book will be dedicated to an in-depth study of the murk-staves as they deserve some focused attention.

If alchemy is about anything, it is about owning up to and removing our impurities, turning weaknesses to strengths, unconsciousness into consciousness and so on. So every rune has two simultaneous sides to be considered -- regardless of whether they can be drawn upside down (like Tiwaz) or not (like Dagaz) -- two polarities, between which is a spectrum, an entire reality.

I cannot so easily separate the positive and the negative from each rune, so I have included commentary on both aspects within the rune meaning itself. It is far from complete. My advice is to consider the dark as well as the light of any rune, and so much the better if you can transcend this duality altogether, and consider the dark and light as inseparable.

Lastly, carry this book around with you. I'm not suggesting that you learn through osmosis, but I know from long experience that certain books are wonderful companions to have with you. I have designed this book to be not only a reference book on the runes, but to provide insight, wisdom and inspiration that may act as a catalyst for your own creations and breakthroughs. Trust me when I say they can take place at any moment.

Consciousness and the Unconscious

I will use the terms 'conscious' and 'unconscious' a lot in my work, but not as opposites. Consciousness emerges from unconsciousness, which emerges from proto-consciousness (things that are neither conscious, nor unconscious, but prior to those, such as animated non-living reactive processes).

Consciousness is a process by which something that was previously unconscious is transmuted into an active power, rather than a reactive power. We are generally aware of something conscious, whereas we are not as easily aware of the unconscious, and often project it out onto our environment -- refusing to adopt it as it is in truth: a part of ourselves.

Consciousness is much more a process of continuous transmutation than a 'state' necessarily higher or superior to unconsciousness. A bad habit, for instance, is changed first by becoming fully aware of it, and consciously and persistently correcting it, until it has changed into a good habit -- a new habit chosen by you, consciously. The good habit is trained until it once again becomes unconscious.

We are also unconscious when we sleep. Clearly there is nothing wrong with sleep -- we need to be unconscious sometimes. The unconscious in this sense signifies dreams, intuitions, archetypes, imagination. Conscious awareness -- that is our perception and senses -- is riddled with bias and errors that can be discovered and accounted for. Many of these errors come from the complex interplay between our conscious self and unconscious self. We are never all conscious or all unconscious, but both at once. We remember fragments of our lives in our sleep, and fragments of our dreams in our waking lives. We may remember our past, but not all of it at once.

I write all this is to dissuade the reader from mistakenly interpreting my use of the words 'consciousness' and 'the unconscious' as opposites, or as a moral matter, simply because of the limits of the language. It is true that conflicts sometimes exist between the conscious and the unconscious, but not always. Rune alchemy aims to further our ability to transmute an unconscious process into a conscious one for the purposes of discovery, understanding and change. The cultivation of 'awareness' is only one part of a grander scheme.

THE RUNE MEANINGS

THE FIRST AETT

The first Aett is concerned with the human dimension within the context of society. The rune secrets it holds deal with our personal awakening and integration into an awakening community. Once we can activate these energies properly as part of our being, we will then have the knowledge and power to profoundly shape ourselves.

Fehu - "Cattle"

KEY CONCEPTS: mobility, beginnings, wealth, luck, charisma, initial conditions, baggage, debt, ownership, freedom, non-violence

To the ancients, cattle represented a sort of mobile wealth that had to be nurtured. It also represents something less pleasant, and that is the idea of our own position, according to the wealth we were born into, or begin with, as we awaken to our study of the runes.

We all begin as cattle, as one of the herd. There are always pressures to fit in and follow. It is tempting to assume that we are autonomous. In the beginning though, we are just another person, and we are much more 'like everyone else' than we know. In some ways this is a good thing, in many ways, it is a bad thing. If we seek the independence and freedom that we deserve, we must accept this starting point and work from there.

So to begin the path of the runes, we are concerned with our initial condition and the luck we have had, or not had, up until that point. When we first begin to become conscious of ourselves, we see that there is much in our lives that seems to be our 'default' -- a given. It was not put there by us consciously -- so in essence we do not 'own' it. We simply carry it as baggage, or debt, or chains which immobilize us and prevent more consciously created circumstances.

Luck is just a kind of innate ability to deal with meaningless disorder. Until we take control of ourselves our circumstances are essentially luck of the draw, formed by our position in the herd and the conditioning that the herd imposes upon us. We have had good luck, or bad luck -- but it is all the same. We do not own our own destiny.

This initial, inherited luck, is a power known as "Hamingja", a kind of gravitas or charisma. It is increased through acts of courage and honor; the pursuit of truth. Charisma is essentially our 'likability' and it is the first trait that emerges from within that can influence our luck. Charisma is our ability to adapt to and exploit social situations on the fly.

The magic of influencing our luck depends on how we use our luck to consciously build our initial conditions. The more our conditions are actively and positively constructed, the better our 'luck' will become, as it emerges from within us, and from the situations we naturally create for ourselves -- whether we know it or not. Luck is not indifferent chance. Chance comes from outside, and luck from within.

Wealth can be defined in many ways. The simplest and most contemporary measure is money. It is better to think about it in terms of ability to blunt necessity and to extend one's personal power over the universe. Money is a trivial concern next to this latter, truer wealth.

Fehu challenges us to think differently about wealth, and about ownership and debt. Ownership could be viewed as a form of violence. It requires force on the fringes of any system that makes it central, and that force alienates rather than integrates, separates rather than unifies. In large systems, like nations, it causes war and poverty, so the violence of ownership is very real.

Money, as it exists in today's world, is debt -- and when we need money, when our actions revolve around getting money, we see that our actions are not free. To become free, we think we need money, and we are taught to accumulate wealth by this system's rules. Then, in getting money, we are absorbed into a system in which nothing is free. What we own, ends up owning us.

The secret of Fehu is that real wealth is a type of freedom. Ownership and money are illusions at this level of wealth. When we define wealth as freedom, we can see the chains of our modern world much more clearly. This is a powerful step in separating ourselves from the herd.

We can start over whenever we want. We are much less rooted to one place than we believe. We can pick up and go. We can start every day new. We can even harness this energy to make every minute count.

The first thing to be free from is our limiting past. Our baggage. Our debt. Starting fresh, we immediately recreate the majority of our initial conditions. You can feel this fresh start in your body, it is very real. This is among the secrets of Fehu.

The energy of Fehu flows from dependence on the herd toward independence as an individual. When we seek such independence, it is a movement both into ourselves and outward into the world. We intend to learn the way of freedom. By the end of the First Aett, the rune Wunjo, we return to bring the joy of this freedom into human communities, generating a new, exponential cycle of authentic wealth, and we do so non-violently.

Uruz - "Auroch"

KEY CONCEPTS: manifestation, self-preservation, persistence, raw primal power, survival, physical growth, archetypal patterning, organic structure, formative life force, immediate action, permanence

The Auroch was a beast that symbolizes the principle of Uruz at work in our lives. It is a relative of the cattle, but wild and primal. To pass from the unconsciousness and dependence of childhood into the independence of adulthood, the individual must confront and best Uruz, the Auroch. Once upon a time, this was done as an actual test of might and courage against a living breathing Auroch. In our times, the Auroch is extinct, and it is we who are the beast.

Uruz is the rune of becoming. It is the rune of immediate action, in the physical and organic world. When a thought becomes a physical thing, it is being manifested through some means, into a reality. Through the secrets of Uruz we can shape our body, our environment, our habits and the structure of our brain.

This is our primitive, animal self. There is much of us that is not human. It is the messy, primal truth. The shit, sweat, sex, and hunger. The blood and guts and violence. No one is always above these things, nor is it necessarily wise to be. The messy organic reality of things is never quite as 'perfect' as we would like it to be.

Uruz is part self-preservation. It is the force that prevents you from jumping off a bridge or stepping in front of a car. It is the force that prevents you from stabbing your hand with a knife. It is a strong force, a heavy force. Doing strange things was not good for survival, so as life evolved, so did the routines that embed habit, conditioning, tradition and conformity. Uruz is like a center of gravity that stubbornly holds us to our accumulated patterns.

Uruz is the force that makes us grow from children to adults. It takes food and transmutes it into useful material for our body's essential structure. Uruz is also behind our habits and the basic mechanisms that allow us to copy the behavior of others, learn or invent new behaviors, and train ourselves athletically. We are usually conditioned unconsciously, but we can condition ourselves consciously, once we know how.

Uruz represents our genetic inheritance. It is the blueprint upon which our life force is based. Although there is a huge amount of wiggle room, we will constantly be confronted by the power of Uruz, as it acts to physically bind us to our old patterns, our physical blueprint, our habits and conditioning. Uruz is the pressure of conformity, of habit, of automation, reflex, and instinct. This is a sticky, stubborn force. It is territorial. It does not respond gently to being challenged.

Strangely, the conformity found on the surface of Uruz, which often contributes to territorial disputes and feuds between individuals and groups, is contrasted by the opposing reality that we are nearly genetically uniform as a species, despite the flourishes that make us unique.

You will notice that both Fehu in its focus on wealth and freedom and Uruz in its focus on health and habit both point toward extremely basic concerns that most of us spend an incredible amount of our time occupied with. When they are neglected, we soon come to ruin. They, like the other runes of this Aett, are fundamental human concerns, always at work in our mind -- important mysteries to be experienced and unlocked.

Uruz is a rune that can be understood, and harnessed. It represents the Auroch, which is to be overcome and mastered as a rite of passage into adulthood. The Auroch is a metaphor for grabbing the beast by the horns and taking control. Therefore, Uruz represents the indomitable human will, strength, courage and backbone, but also its blind, two-sided nature. We have all allowed, in some way, our own unconscious conditioning, our disempowering beliefs to grow into powerful and intimidating beasts.

Yet once harnessed, the secret of Uruz can make dreams into physical reality in the same way it slowly and surely persisted in making your body. But it takes work and perseverance to master because it is the embodiment of work and perseverance.

The energy of Uruz flows around the self, binding us to our biological form, fixing our patterns and giving us permanence, but the cost is that we form habits and conditioning that can be difficult to shed.

Thurisaz - "Giants"

KEY CONCEPTS: constructive conflict, technology, self-defense, innovation, struggle against unconscious forces, enthusiasm, self-empowerment, breaking down resistance, tactical thought, protection, battle.

The Giants, also known as Thurses, represented the unconscious resistance to the arising of consciousness (Asgard) in the universe. Evolutionarily speaking, this rune symbolizes our rise from our unconscious, conditioned selves into our human potential, and bespeaks of the inevitable conflicts that result within and without, as this rise occurs.

Like Thor, who is like a Giant himself, and his Hammer, used against the Giants, Thurisaz is the rune that represents our tools and technologies, whether they be physical or mental in nature. They are used to develop the proto-consciousness and control the unconsciousness that remains within us or around us -- managing and outsmarting, though not necessarily vanquishing or defeating. The power of Thurisaz is on the borderline, the frontier of our expansion, and the cutting edge of technology.

Thurisaz is like the strike of lightning that smashes through a specific problem, or the thunderclap of powerful realization. Its power is targeted toward specific problems within the unconscious, and its energy transmutes the problem toward its solution. It is about identifying and fixing our problems. It has a feeling backed by enthusiasm and purpose.

Thurisaz is the innovative, problem-solution matrix that is constantly at work within humans. Taking control of how we define our problems, and how we structure our pursuit of solutions, is a powerful and effective practice. Yet the fact remains that we create problems for ourselves if we leave this power unattended, and like a neglected garden, the source of our fruitfulness can slip back into the wild from which we emerged. This is because it is a raw elemental force that channels through from our inner power, a brutal power when uncontrolled. Can anyone doubt man's destructive potential in an age where our planet is cloaked in a nuclear umbrella? Or when we have the capacity to slay one another? These grim potentials lay unconscious within all of us. They are the Giants.

This rune harkens to the enthusiasm for mastering our environment. Where Uruz represents our biological growth, Thurisaz is our natural tendency toward technological growth. Humans construct niches for themselves so effectively that we have transformed the very face of the planet -- we are a force of nature, and always have been. However, there is often little consciousness involved in our impacts.

We harness the secret of Thurisaz when we make conscious adjustments to our immediate environment in order to influence emerging situations. We do this naturally for our children, or for any we wish to shelter, defend or protect, but we can forget to do it for ourselves. Our environment can both disempower us, or reinforce our abilities.

Strategic and tactical thinking enters on this level, signified by the thorn or spike shape to Thurisaz. This enables us to outsmart the brute strength that lay within Uruz or the force of unconsciousness within ourselves, and around us. The more force used upon the thorn, the more damage the thorn does back. The thorn, though passive, is active in shaping behavior indirectly. Though do not mistake Thurisaz as a passive power. This is just one manifestation of its potential, a form of protection, threat and warning.

We also have a psychological environment formed by our unexamined assumptions and beliefs. This can work for us or against us, so Thurisaz can be used to meditate upon these mental attitudes, and one by one, find more empowering substitutes for them.

Thurisaz jumps on problems as they occur, often striking the root of a perceived thing and ignoring the important subtleties and details. This is a disadvantage in relying too heavily on the rune that quickly leads to its murk-stave (reversed) implications. Aside from being impulsive, and quick to anger, our untrained mind often creates problems where there are none, and every solution seems to cause more problems. It is tactical more than strategic, seeing a battle but not the war. Thurisaz is excellent at addressing the short term, but can be nearly blind when peering further into the future.

Hidden within Thurisaz are the secret laws surrounding the use of force -- it causes more problems than it solves, and those problems cannot often be solved by the mentality which was responsible for their creation.

The energy of Thurisaz is much like lightning, striking specific problem points as they are realized. It can send that same tingle up our spine. The realization is much like thunder, very audible. And just like nature, the lightning of change may have to happen before the thunder of realization is perceived.

Ansuz - "A god"

KEY CONCEPTS: order, breath, gods, evolution, communication, reason, inspiration, poetry, music, intellect, logos

Ansuz refers to a god as an animating principle associated with inspiration and communication. This rune signifies the mental gifts that make us uniquely human, and the aspects of humanity that we pass down not through blood, but through breath -- ideas rather than physical things.

There is a higher ordering to Ansuz, easily compared to something 'divine'. It is our human instinct to order, to pattern and to name. But the power of Ansuz lay in turning these instincts into conscious powers. It suggests not merely that our gods are only ideas, but that our ideas are our gods. Through this rune we can emulate their ways. This is something to contemplate deeply as we delve further into the secrets within the rune's meaning.

The rune refers to that within us which is capable of transmuting our unmastered but distinctly human abilities into conscious powers of reasoning, storytelling, suggestion, persuasion and poetry. There is a massive amount of awareness to be gained by increasing our ability to speak, listen, read and write. Communication of symbols, as well as transmission and manipulation of meaning lay at the core of this mindset.

Ansuz represents the civilizing tendency of language. It is well known that writing was key to the development of early civilizations. Ansuz represents that step in our evolution when we began to project symbols into our environment in order to alter the psychological meaning of innately meaningless events and objects. These ancient symbols, as they arose in various forms and separate cultures, appeared as powerful arcane magic to the uninitiated and indeed have managed to hold our fascination for thousands of years. The Elder Futhark is one such set of symbols.

These kinds of symbols had incredible power when they first began to be used -- people held them in awe, and they still have power. In English, much of the 'magic' has been sucked out of the characters and symbols, but we still call forming words "spelling" as if to unconsciously acknowledge it as a magical act, the equivalent of casting a spell. We are surrounded by the "logos" of organizations -- Logos being an important term in philosophy, psychology and religion -- originally meaning 'speech', and coming to represent, among the Greeks, the principles of order and knowledge.

The order that we generate because of our pattern-creating minds is one of our most powerful gifts, so powerful, in fact, that we cannot help but seek order in an otherwise chaotic world. Because of this, Ansuz does not simply mean 'a god', it marks our tendency to create the appearance of gods. Likewise it also marks a tendency to place meaning on the most chance events in order to organize and represent them as part of a narrative or cosmology. This ongoing process creates our gods, whether we call them that or not.

All communication is a form of translation. We have a personal set of symbols and meanings, which need to be translated into an agreed language that we share with others, and use to change or persuade one another's viewpoints, mental states and mindsets -- for better or for ill. Conscious symbols are used to transmute unconsciousness into consciousness, and is at the core of alchemy. Ansuz is the alchemy of symbols, using meaning and inspiration to transform our view of the world, which in turn allows us to behave and act differently, and influence the attitudes of those around us.

Becoming conscious of the energy that Ansuz adds to the human situation is a concrete step in allowing us to transcend the culture we were born into and the symbols that limit us. Instead of being continually persuaded and influenced by the ideas of others, we take back our original genius and create our own personal cultural center, which spreads outward into the world. This is what those who created the runes tapped into, and what all of us possess within us.

We can all too easily find ourselves tangled in a web of perplexity as persuasion turns to manipulation, as words are used to conceal actions. Our symbols and words are quite capable of moving us either toward consciousness or unconsciousness. As with all runes, Ansuz has a darker side, filled with riddles, lies and confusion. Even with the best of intentions, if we succumb to esoteric, exclusive language, if we do not demand clarity, if we repeat what we hear thoughtlessly, we are doomed to be caught up in the hypnotic and intoxicating power of Ansuz. To move out of the labyrinth of symbols and meanings, we must turn to other runes.

Raidho - "Ride"

KEY CONCEPTS: the journey, taking action, decision-making, inner compass, nobility held by merit, innate knowledge of right and wrong, psychological narrative, street smarts, common sense

Raidho means 'to ride', as in to journey. The journey is more important than the destination, and it is no good living our lives in order to achieve our happiness 'someday'. We must also move past mistakes and leave obstacles behind, never carrying with us the baggage we accumulate because of error and frustration. Centering our lives around the present moment while taking that next necessary step every day is a core secret we can take away from Raidho.

Raidho represents the essential psychological narrative form. It is why our dreams and our experience seems to string together into a story form that can be retold. But Raidho is not merely the desire to retell a story. Raidho is the pressure within all of us to live a life rather than watch life from a distance as it passes us by. Ansuz tells the stories, Raidho lives them.

Following one's heart and exploring oneself and the world is also a great aspect of this rune. It represents the journey we undertake to find ourselves, to know our loves in life, to follow our dreams, and to leave our roots -- and baggage -- behind. Raidho leaves the words and representations of Ansuz behind and states boldly that "actions are louder than words." Its principles are understood in action, in movement. It is the point at which simple reactions and reflexes give way to authentic, spontaneous action directed by our will. It is powerful, mobile and liberating.

The magic of Raidho revolves around merit rather than persuasion or popularity. When something "speaks for itself", we are referring to just such directness. The power of leading by example is inherent to Raidho, and as such this rune has been associated with leadership and nobility. It is a nobility not bestowed from above, but conferred by deed.

The discovery of flow is an inevitability with this rune, because when we let go of our past limits, and center ourselves in the moment to do that which we love doing, we transcend the passage of time and enter a kind of peak state. This energy, the core of Raidho, allows us to forget the past, forget ourselves and forget the future. We are joyful in the journey, consumed in the current step. We flow and dance and play with the universe in this state. We blend with our personal rhythms, and the rhythms of the world around us. We are experiencing a narrative directly, prior to embellishment.

Raidho helps us discover the natural limits, or laws, of the universe, by running us up against them, alongside them. We learn by doing, picking up necessary information as we go. We learn, moreover, that there are far less limits than we may have first imagined, and the ones that we encounter and train ourselves against, are negotiable.

Street-smarts are a brand of wisdom that Raidho inherently cultivates, because the secret of Raidho is to desolve what we've been told and experience the reality beneath for ourselves, for better or for worse. It can be a painful process for some -- but it is a beautiful and freeing power that really heightens our awareness and strengthens our character.

Awakening Raidho's power within us allows us to make concrete decisions in the present moment and follow them with immediate and massive action. It rips us from our conditioning and habits, propelling us forward to our future selves. It confronts the present moment, challenging us to expect the unexpected, and to do the undoable.

Life is in a constant state of change, of evolution. Environments are continually in flux. The universe is movement. Nothing stands still. When we join this movement, we are set within the current of reality, and we ride that current toward whatever reality has in store for us to discover.

This rune's flow of energy surges forward. It is the energy of movement and change. Harnessing it consciously allows us to take control of our destiny from the unconscious factors that would have us float idly to and fro with the tide, allow us to stagnate, or circle in a whirlpool current.

It is when Raidho is reactive, rather than active, that its reversed or murk-stave comes clear. When we are forced to move, or go with the flow but fail to invoke our most noble qualities, we are destined to find that our journey has no destination -- that our past and future haunt us with their uncertainty. We float in the darkness, unknown, unable to take in any of the sights. We are unaware of the context through which we travel, and bump up against rocky shores rather than sailing into harbor. Often it is not obvious right away that we have taken a wrong turn in our journey, and Raidho's momentum can be troublesome to reverse and set right. There are many deeds which cannot be undone. It is good to have knowledge of the path ahead, for which we turn to another rune.

Kenaz - "Torchlight"

KEY CONCEPTS: Knowledge, art, learning, teaching, discovery, science, research, illumination, traditional lore, observation, cognitive faculty, quest for truth, cunning, craft

Kenaz represents torchlight, our ability to harness fire for warmth, light and crafting. The torch and hearth, old concepts for us now, have developed certain associations which we will explore in depth. Kenaz also represents the forge, the fire of crafting. In the context of following Raidho, Kenaz can signify a lighthouse or signal fire -- something to guide the journeyer safely on their way.

Ken means 'to know' in many related languages.

Kenaz is a rune of kinship, discovery and illumination. The torch lights the hallways of the mind's keep. The hearth warms a million homes, and generation upon generation gathered around these fires to pass on stories and lore, to ward off the darkness of ignorance, to keep culture alive.

Kenaz, in one way, represents the knowledge of a generation, being passed along and added to by a contemporary generation. Some progress is inevitable due to this passing down of knowledge, but so is inter-generational conflict and the passing down of stifling traditions, superstition and limiting world views. The successful resolution of the generation gap is a wisdom unique to Kenaz.

Kenaz is also representative of the forge, where our knowledge can be applied to craft our tools. But this rune speaks of a metaphysical forge, the one under whose flame, hammer and anvil we can turn ourselves into living, breathing works of art, sharpen our minds into powerful instruments, and remove impurities from our spirits.

It has long been said that knowledge is power, and that the truth will set you free. This is perhaps because knowledge of reality is the most powerful awareness we can have. But what does knowledge of the truth free us from, and what new responsibilities must we live up to once we discover it? All authentic magic as well as all authentic science springs from the sacrifices we make to understand the universe and align our actions with its laws. Freedom is not simply doing whatever we wish.

We shape ourselves by understanding the craft. Kenaz is the rune of understanding a process, and applying it to create. It results in both science and art -- and magic.

Kenaz grants us access to our inner-forge, where we may deconstruct our illusions, beliefs and habits to create ourselves anew. It guides us back to our inner hearth, where we may take comfort and become the crafters and artists of our own culture.

Kenaz helps us uncover the stories of our origins and our place in the universe. It is a rune of tried and tested cause and effect. If you know that a cause produces certain effects, you can predict the future more accurately. But cause and effect are meaningless without experimentation. The scientific method must always be utilized. It is tempting to assume cause and effect show causation, when it only shows correlation.

Knowledge of truth has often been vilified as occult, and yet it is the most noble of pursuits. It is the chief aim of both science and justice. Only those whose interests lay heavily vested in keeping others ignorant will attack the people and institutions who represent the search of knowledge and truth. Yet it is a futile struggle on behalf of the ignorant: knowledge of truth shall forever prevail. Knowledge of truth is open to anyone who is courageous enough to align with it. Knowledge of truth fears nothing and is threatened by none. It is invincible!

The energy of Kenaz flows from illumination toward investigating hidden regions. It manifests as our desire to learn, to teach and to know the truth. We feel the fire it represents very strongly when we discover we've been lied to, and that fire fuels the further pursuit of truth, as well as its defense and propagation into the world. We are naturally averse to secrecy -- we know intuitively that secrecy runs counter to the aims of truth and justice. The murk stave of Kenaz could represent the darkness of ignorance, and the blind superstition and paranoia that transpires in the human mind when immersed in less illuminated states.

Gebo - "Gift"

KEY CONCEPTS: Gifting, giving, receiving, exchange, positive bonds, gratitude, reciprocity, balance, unspoken debt, inborn talents, sacrifice, sacred marriage

A gift demands a gift, they say, and so Gebo, though it literally means 'gift', is not all about giving. It is about receiving, exchange and reciprocity -- spiritual debt, rather than as we know it today -- and the types of bonds these actions create. These bonds are important, and we find ourselves sharply defined by them, both personally, and collectively as a society.

The act of giving is a subtle, unspoken art-form. To bring it into consciousness is to gain greatly. With nothing to lose, we have all to gain -- to reach this state, we give our all. Courtesy and respect cost nothing, and should always be given. This does not mean, however, that you are not doing someone a favor by challenging them when they step out of line. One aught not reward someone for undeserving behavior.

Basic reciprocity is at the heart of our interactions with one another. Gebo could be seen as the domain of economics, from the smallest exchange to the sum total of all exchanges. As a society we decide what things should be public, and what private. We agree on our rules for ownership, and compensation.

Unlike the mobile property (or money) of Fehu, Gebo is about the rules of the exchange: the responsibilities and the etiquette. As we saw with Fehu, ownership can potentially generate conflict and violence at the fringes of the system it creates -- concentrating wealth into the hands of a few, leading to tyranny, oppression, poverty and war in the world.

In the economy of the gift, equality and equilibrium is maintained by circulating ownership fairly, through sharing and gifting. Taken a step further, ownership is absent, gifting impossible, so gifts become creations that improve and delight the world, freely accessible to all. This is the ideal inherent in the Gebo rune.

We also give of ourselves, whether in service, charity or love. We must do so freely, without the need to receive in return. Of course the truth is, that you need to receive compensation where it is due. Recognizing when to collect a reward for a job well done is part of the art of gifting. Gebo is about the unspoken contracts we make with one another, yet must be reflected upon and honored if we are to find harmony. Mutual gain and shared wealth are the hallmarks of wisdom in matters like these.

The murk-stave aspect of Gebo could be embodied in the image of the powerful, destructive dragon sitting atop a hoard of gold and treasure. Incapable of creation, fixated on accumulation, we can see that the dragon is perhaps not as mythical as we should suppose.

Gebo is also concerned with the sacrifices we must incur in order to give something truly valuable to the world. We must sacrifice when we wish to exchange our present self for a new and improved future self. So Gebo teaches of how to let go, how to give up, how to sacrifice, because all of that is part of gifting.

There is another sacrificial aspect to Gebo, and that has to do with giving yourself completely to one another in a relationship. Many of us strongly feel the desire to search for the perfect partner, a lover, a husband or wife. This search is best accomplished by realizing your end of the bargain.

If you want to be given the gift of a sacred marriage, you have to be as perfect as the person you want to be with. You can't fool your sacred partner. You need to be someone worthy of their true love, as they are worthy to be yours. This is the sacrifice of the sacred marriage exchange. We must sacrifice our pettiness and know that there are always sacrifices to be made when this kind of bond is formed with a lover. Understanding that these sacrifices lead to a combined wealth greater than could be attained alone is key. And we must know whether a relationship actually is leading to greater wealth, rather than turmoil and resentment.

Gebo also teaches us that we all have a mysterious gift, a part of ourselves that must be discovered, a talent that must be turned into a skill, before we can effectively take control of our destiny. To shirk this gift is to neglect the debt we have to Life for the life it has given us. It is a real debt, one whose weight we always feel within us. By embracing our inner gift, we can generate and create unique and beautiful new things in the world in order to give back. This repays the debt, and more -- it creates true wealth.

Remember, gratitude is a power to be reckoned with. Gratitude can even be invoked when we have the opportunity to give. Some people are grateful for every breath, and the air gives of itself freely to all. Be like the fresh air to people and you will embrace the secrets of Gebo.

Unconsciously, our mind often focuses on the negative and we remember our painful experiences more readily than our good ones. We can accumulate resentments instead of gratitude. Consciously cultivate the habit of doing just the opposite, and the universe will flood you with more gifts, as if it were attracted to your gratitude like gravity.

Wunjo - "Joy"

KEY CONCEPTS: Fellowship, harmonious groups, leadership, connection, understanding, celebration of life, play

Wunjo is a rune that recognizes joy as our most powerful human desire. We all want happiness, we feel that everyone deserves happiness. If we find that someone is unhappy, we instinctively know that they deserve the hope of a better life. We are genuinely concerned for the well-being of others. Despite what some people think, most people are caring and wish they understood the roots of suffering so that they could alleviate it all around them.

Connecting with people we love is something that really brings joy into our hearts, and we are saddened whenever there is a falling out, or death.

Wunjo is commonly interpreted as the joy that emerges from meaningful face to face connections with family, friends and community; in other words, the tribe. It is also the movement of energy into the realm of the unknown: the excitement and freshness of meeting new friends, and experiencing different ways of life. It is strangers able to smile freely at one another. Its energy can sometimes be felt as a 'click' when two people meet and suddenly see eye to eye.

It is also something more fundamental: the joy of just being. To be alive is enough.

In our age, we are each leaders of tribes. We manage contacts and a variety of relationships. When we choose our friends carefully, we are consciously shaping ourselves. No one is able to remain unchanged by deep connections with other people, so cultivating positive connections with positive people is a great task in life. It seems unfair to select some over others, but our happiness depends on it.

Wunjo as a murk-stave represents the manifestation of aggressive tribalism, pressures of conformity, group insecurity, hostility toward other groups or outsiders, gossip -- and the whole host of human issues that lead away from the joyful celebration of one another's diversity, forever enjoyed by free people. It can represent personal and national depression, a lack of joy in life, often as a consequence of these other symptoms of social degradation.

Creating or mending the relationships between people is an important task. This is the great art of a healthy community. The nurturance of a more stable state of universal content is the hallmark of Wunjo's secret power, and provides the base state for joy to most easily emerge from.

Wunjo is also the domain of shared identity, conveyed in culture, traditions and art. When art and tradition fall too heavily under neglect, the culture unravels and stagnates, the communities become joyless and our work seems mundane and pointless. We toil for future promises of safety while our communities and culture fall apart. Fun is replaced by work. There are less uplifting experiences to be had, fewer positive states to be shared. So Wunjo is a very social energy, and affects the texture of our every day relationships.

The secret of this rune is that joy and freedom go hand in hand. To realize this, we need to have "free time" as a focus in our lives. The reversal of Wunjo's power often comes with isolation and a conspicuous lack of time and flexibility in one's work. Wunjo is an excess of energy that spends itself living life as a celebration, every day as your first and your last, and adopting as family any friend who enters your life. Spontaneous creativity emerges from such play. We see it among children, or in the friendly battles of wits between young adults, or the wise teaching of our elders. Life is good. Wunjo is to know and feel this above and despite everything. It is the lightness of being, which children tend to have. It is a powerful form of freedom.

SECOND AETT

The second Aett explores our human relationship with universal principles that are inimical to our human situation. Many of the runes in this row point toward realities that exists in spite of us, not because of us, and often enough, come into conflict with our wishes. By understanding these principles, we can adjust our own ways to align with the stark realities that life places upon us, and in turn, gain the power and freedom that is our birthright.

Hagalaz - "Hail"

KEY CONCEPTS: crisis, catastrophe, hardship, the indifference of nature, chaos, radical change, unavoidable unpleasantness, the unalterable, acceptance, surrender, courage

Hagalaz is the first rune in the ordering that really stands out as a negative one. Many people try to put a positive spin on Hagalaz, but Hagalaz transcends our sense of morality, right or wrong, good or bad. It doesn't care, it doesn't make sense, and it can be exceptionally violent. Hagalaz, at its core, is that which we cannot change. We are the ones that change.

Hagalaz is a rune that symbolizes a powerful fact about the world: that what we generally consider nature is actually a fragile equilibrium between unimaginable catastrophes. The explosion of stars, super massive black holes, ice ages, comets that cause mass extinctions, hail that wipes out crops and starves whole communities, storms at sea that sink ships; Hagalaz is the first in a row of runes that represent the inhuman indifference of the universe.

By virtue of its meaningless and inimical twists, some who deserve reward receive instead ruin, while the wicked may sometimes prosper. Hagalaz is the stormy temper of the future, which has no care for our best laid plans, nor for our notions of justice. It is the past that haunts us, and the present that locks us into this moment.

For the most part, Hagalaz always refers to power that is beyond our ability as humans to harness. We may toy with certain powers as we become technologically sophisticated in the centuries to come, but it is an open debate as to whether we can even control our own propensity to innovate, and whether we can keep from destroying ourselves. In our age, mass society has become a force of nature. Hagalaz can even represent nuclear war or catastrophic global climate change brought by human actions.

The events that are the hallmark of Hagalaz are always dramatic, even if we know it may be so only to us, personally. A breakup with a loved one, a death in the family, a turn of luck that brings radical change for better or for worse. These events give us tremendous pause and sometimes we must begin again from the beginning, embracing the opportunity to have a clean slate -- however painful.

Our response to the energy Hagalaz brings into our lives tells us a lot about ourselves. The world will make us or break us according to how able we are to carry on in spite of its profound indifference.

Gaining power over this energy does not mean commanding storms, nor becoming a sole agent of radical change. It lay in accepting that which we cannot change -- adapting where we can, and surrendering where we cannot. It means avoiding victim-consciousness and maintaining grace and integrity under immense pressure. It means courage and defiance in the face of the impossible.

Hagalaz is a reminder to us that certain things, as catastrophic as they may be, are not worth worrying about. It is a great gift to reflect the indifference of nature back at itself. If that comet heading for Earth doesn't care about you, why should you care about it? It is not personal. It is Hagalaz.

Psychologically, Hagalaz is about the objective confrontation with our own, personal catastrophe: the unconscious patterns of our past. It is an immense act of awakening to forgive your past, to accept it as an act of nature, and to realize that there is nothing you can do to change what has been. You can only move forward toward consciousness from this point. The past happened to you, and it was real, and you have to deal with its consequences... but it was like a disaster, a catastrophe. Forgive it. You can do nothing about what happened, only what will happen now.

This forgiving of the unalterable is a force of radical change in and of itself, and it is the secret that Hagalaz reveals to us. When we stop repressing the dark side, the negative, stop living according to our past and fearing our future, we actually become whole. We realize that there is nothing we cannot weather. Even death may lead us to the golden halls of Valhalla.

The energy of Hagalaz is like that of a hurricane passing through us and over us, and yet afterward, we remain.

Nauthiz - "Need"

KEY CONCEPTS - Necessity, need-fire, resistance, constraint, conflict, effort, hard work, life lessons, force of growth, consequence of past action, pain, doing what must be done, neglect

The second rune of the second Aett also challenges the student who would seek to impose their positive bias upon the meaning of the runes. Nauthiz is often bleak and universally indifferent to human desire. Of course, respecting the reality it points to ensures that we do not violate its laws.

The first obvious interpretation of Nauthiz is that it represents that which is necessity. Not what we desire, or wish, but what we actually need, as an absolute. It is the energy behind our needs, and represents the part of us which is ultimately non-negotiable. You need air to breathe, food to eat, study to learn, and love to grow. Our needs bind our form to the forms of the universe, and represent the limits of the self. All humans must have these things in order to survive.

We notice immediately when deprived of our most basic needs, but others are more subtle and more easily ignored. The secret Nauthiz reveals to us is how to look at things through the lens of our needs, the essential, rather than the desirable, the latter which can lead to fantasy.

Nauthiz represents the inevitability of human suffering as our desires come into conflict with the needs that the harsh realities of life impose upon us. Our desires, wishes and fantasies often lead to dramatic conflicts with our needs. We seem to have an endless capacity to wish something were so, when it is not, or to think we need one thing, when we actually need something entirely different.

But conflict with our desires is not the only conflict implicit in the energy of Nauthiz. Our needs have conflicts with each other! We need the company of others, but also time to ourselves. We need safety and security, but also uncertainty and adventure. Our habits pull us one way, even when we know we must change them. We also differ from one another in that some need more or less of something than others -- frustrating our efforts to find good advice.

Our needs are the parts of us most linked to the universe, most connected to the unalterable. When we run up against them, we are challenging our limits, and ultimately those limits will win. This resistance is necessary, for without it, our form would fall apart. We are a part of the universe, held up by it. Limits define and formulate. The illusion that we end at our skin makes us forget that we are deeply connected to the world around us, and that certain laws do rule our personal destiny.

Meeting with necessity is hard. Sometimes we are stuck between a rock and a hard place. We have to choose between two seeming evils. There are such things as lose-lose situations. And in such times, we must simply do what needs be done. The secret of Nauthiz lay in resolving inevitable conflicts, in identifying one's own needs and the needs of others, and using such conflicts and necessities to our advantage rather than allowing them to cause havoc in our lives through neglecting them.

Nauthiz energy flows outward from necessity. It is a constraining energy, only temporarily negotiable. It reminds us to identify our needs and insure that they are being met. When this energy is ignored for too long it can bring about toil and suffering. When it is stubbornly neglected, disruption is not far on the horizon.

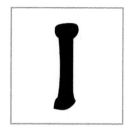

Isa - "Ice"

KEY CONCEPTS: concentration, will and focus, ego-consciousness, self-identity, stillness, stasis, self-preservation

This rune, Isa, points to the fixed perspective of the self, and includes our notions of individuality, willpower and focus. Our ideas about ourselves form our self-identity. Our ability to focus and pay attention are often felt to be the inmost 'I'. All this can be referred to as our ego-consciousness. Ego is a latin term found in psychology and adopted by new age spirituality, which has led to endless confusion.

Our innermost observer is a fixed aspect of the world we live in, so long as we live. It is the common law that every individual is his own self, and that we are never not here, never not now. The universe is, once again, indifferent to any desire on our part to be someone other than who we are. We tread on thin ice when we pretend to be something we are not. Isa can help us construct a healthy ego, or it can lead us toward egomania and deceitfulness.

In a certain sense, Isa is the rune of our center of awareness. It is all our superficial powers of perception, sensory awareness and our ability to direct our will and focus upon certain aspects of our environment. It is also riddled with bias and error, as cognitive psychology has resolutely shown in countless examples.

For this reason, it is a rune of surface appearances. We all know there are treacherous and untold depths beneath the ice, and we are painfully aware that our ability is limited in assessing the safety of ice we wish to cross. We know that icebergs hide much more than they show above the surface of the ocean. Yet we are prone to believing in something uncritically because our senses tell us that it is so, and this is a particular danger when dealing with Isa.

Sensory illusions of all sorts are represented here with Isa, chiefly our own experience of being centered 'around' our experiencer. Yet just as the sun moving through the sky might lead us falsely to believe that the Earth was at the center, the bias of the experiencer is that the world revolves around itself.

We develop a healthy ego by thoroughly knowing ourselves, by limiting our assumptions, and by treading carefully. When we have the self-awareness, we thicken the ice and are less threatened by perceived attacks on our person. We can separate ourselves from the opinions and judgements of others, and transmute stubbornness to willpower, insecurity to confidence, and distraction to quiet focus. We are in control, not easily swayed, capable of breaking down mountains over time, like a glacier.

When we approach meditation through focus on our senses and our breathing, we are tapping into the stillness and calm of Isa. Do not mistake this meditation for something that it is not. We do not transcend the ego simply because we learn to sit still and keep our cool. But it is one path toward developing a healthy and helpful inmost self. This leads us towards seeing through our own thought patterns and becoming aware of the built-in flaws and limits of sense and perception. Meditation reveals us to ourselves, as we learn to watch, or sit still and listen.

Outwardly, Isa represents the harshness of our environment and the hostility of the elements. We are frequently interrupted by the demands of an indifferent universe. Our individual needs breed an ego-centric, selfish orientation -- necessary for survival.

The trouble we confront with Isa is that this ego-centric, selfish orientation is unconscious and reactive even when our survival is not dependent on it being so. We confuse attacks on our identity, or on our ideas, as attacks on our physical person, and act out with the same defensive viciousness if we do not reign ourselves in.

Jera - "Year"

KEY CONCEPTS: time, patience, cycles, harvest, progress, waiting, effort, gentle indifference

Jera most clearly refers to the procession of time, literally meaning 'Year'. Here is the fourth rune in a row that represents the indifference of the universe, in this case, the gentle but inevitable procession of time.

Time marches relentlessly forward. The rhythms of nature are gradual and predictable, and that certainty has been a boon to human progress over the millennia. In fact, it is fundamental to the cycles of most living creatures.

Our lives, too, have their seasons, of youth, adulthood, middle and old age. Time's current pushes us, with magnificent indifference, toward our deaths, which arrive at a time far less predictable than we should like. Though equally inevitable, death is a stark contrast to the slow, predictable rhythms that we are comfortable with. We are fortunate when our end comes due to age, though this entails the sacrifice of watching ourselves, and the world we knew, get old.

Jera is the rune of patience and effort. Herein lay the deepest secret and greatest power of human progress and individual success. Talent and ingenuity may get us so far, but to build something lasting or to harvest a bountiful reward, planning, patience and hard work are the single key ingredients. We must spend our time wisely if we are to have a lasting accomplishment.

We reap what we sow. There is great reward for proper timing and effort. Jera's secrets show us how to build tomorrow today and caution us against borrowing from the future.

Jera represents growth and development, but also decline and erosion over time. Powerful monuments still exist, such as stonehenge, the pyramids, or the Aztec and Inca ruins in South America, yet time has slowly but surely proceeded onward without the people and societies that once maintained them. Artifacts may or may not linger as their creators change or fade away. History is a master at covering its own tracks.

To align oneself with the energy of Jera is to align oneself with this neutral reality -- that one day all that is shall be no more. Jera is thus, a reminder that even our own civilization will someday be ancient, that the future is inevitable, that it can be shaped to an extent, but that on a long enough timeline all memory of it will fade.

It is through Jera's truth that we can partly know the rhythms that the ancients were accustomed to, that were important. But it is also because of Jera that slowly, bit by bit, some knowledge has been lost. At the same time, through the ebbs and flows of the years, knowledge is also re-created and re-constructed. This rune is indiscriminate in its forgetfulness and regrowth, and represents the extent to which gentleness can also be harsh and powerful.

Jera's secret can be harnessed to allow things to pass and be forgotten. It can also be used to summon the patience that hard work requires. They say that good things come to those that wait. What we must wait for is the correct time to act. But a garden doesn't plant itself. Jera is simultaneously the power of hard work, harvest and maintenance -- and its ultimate futility.

Ihwaz - "Yew"

KEY CONCEPTS: The timeless, eternity, mysteries of life and death, the afterlife, immortality, the reality of other worlds, total perspective, solitude, oblivion

I have been told that Ihwaz is one of the most mysterious runes. I believe that this is because Ihwaz represents the mysteries of the universe, themselves, and our initiation into those mysteries. It represents the verticality of the world tree, Yggdrassil, and the nine worlds associated with it. The yew tree is a toxic evergreen, and humans can distill a poison from it. It is the longest living plant in Europe.

Like the other runes of this row, Ihwaz reflects the indifference of the universe, but in a special way. Ihwaz represents access to other worlds and dimensions that are hardly concerned with our petty human affairs.

Ihwaz signifies the reality of other worlds, with other laws, from the quantum, to the molecular, to the cellular, up into the heavens, other planets, stars, galaxies and beyond. This rune exposes us to the total perspective, to infinity. This infinity challenges us to put ourselves into perspective -- a perspective which most of us are terrified of, or unable to even contemplate.

Ihwaz is the vastness of timeless eternity. It represents that which does not and cannot fundamentally change. It is the inevitability of death, but also the inevitability of continuation beyond the threshold of death. The search for immortality has always been the domain of Ihwaz.

Humankind will forever continue to unlock the mysteries represented by Ihwaz, though they are endless in number. Where once we had recourse only to the occult, the methods of science have emerged. Perhaps our future evolution will provide us other ways. Nevertheless, onward to infinity we shall go.

The secrets of the universe reveal themselves to us only through a rigorous dedication on our part, to the truth, above all else. The pursuit of that truth requires unwavering courage. The mysteries themselves do not care who pays attention to them -- their rewards are given neutrally -- and they are not always rewards at all.

When we align to this mysterious Ihwaz energy, we experience ourselves as timeless and eternal. The laws of the universe show us that we cannot be destroyed, not truly, even by death.

The mysteries of the afterlife however, are completely locked to us while we live this life. We cannot know what form our journey past that threshold will take. If we are to look at what science has revealed, we know that molecularly, we transform and re-enter the biosphere in billions of pieces. We know that what we are will eventually be returned to the fires of the sun, only to someday form new suns and new worlds. We know from thermodynamics that no energy is created nor destroyed. We are, literally, indestructible to the very core. It is merely our current form and identity that dies.

Courage is one thing we can take with us to the very brink of oblivion, and so the ancients believed that our courage strongly defined us in this life and determined much of what happened in the beyond, and thus valued it highly. Courageous deeds were considered essential in strengthening one's magical power, and being chosen to join the honorable ranks of fallen warriors in Valhalla.

Ihwaz also represents our fundamental solitude and isolation. It is an existential energy. In our present form, we are harshly alienated from the universe, alone at birth and alone at death. Ihwaz challenges us to transcend this condition through courage and truth-seeking. To be immortal is to be alone, and that we are alone should tell us something when we doubt our immortality.

Our brains seem to implicitly know that other realities with different rules can exist. Neuroplasticity is the key ingredient in its tremendous ability to transform and perceive these realities -- study reveals that we can exist and thrive in totally unknown territory. We see the unfettered diversity inherent in the many cultures that have existed on Earth. What other worlds has our unconscious mind quietly prepared us for?

Whatever lay beyond the threshold, in terms of experience, is locked to us until we are initiated into it by the great unifier of all living beings: death. If there is communication between this world and other dimensions, as some claim, it is through the secrets of this rune.

Perthro - ? - unknown

KEY CONCEPTS: unknown, chance, randomness, meaninglessness, guessing, luck, risk, infinite possibilities, the unknowable, co-incidence

The meaning of Perthro is unknown. Rather than suppose the meaning is lost, treat this as intentional: Perthro represents that which is unknowable and meaningless in the universe. It is the symbolic equivalent of a blank rune.

The idea that we are here by chance, that the universe is random, that not all things have causes, that co-incidence can often be meaningless, that even our most precise mathematics are fundamentally based on our best guess about the nature of things -- all this is intolerable to most people. Our minds rebel against the idea.

Perthro represents once again, the indifference of the universe toward our attempts to know it, to explain it and to give it meaning. If there is an absolute truth, it is unknowable, however many mysteries we uncover and solve. Where Ihwaz represents a mystery to be solved, it is an error to consider Perthro as representing a mystery. Perthro is the unknowable. Something that is solved, or solvable, is not Perthro, which is unsolvable. It is that which we do not even know we do not know. This rune solidly stands in the abyss beyond the human mind's utmost capabilities.

Perthro also represents the nameless, that which cannot be spoken of because it defies our attempts to understand and know and explain. As a consequence it also represents the immeasurable and the unmanifest. It is emptiness. It is nothingness.

Perthro is the domain of chance and events without causation. The fact that we cannot reliably predict the future, that we must guess and take risks, turns all of our lives into a gamble.

Perthro frames the makeup of the universe as uncompromisingly playful. The way to deal with this is to realize life is, in a sense, a sort of high-stakes game. We can transform our life's work into play. This is the connection of Perthro to the lot-cup, to gambling and dice. At a deeper level, we are constantly involved in a game of chance, with luck as its basis. Therefore, Perthro magic involves our powers of guessing. Though there may be ways of improving our odds, remember that chance is still the domain of unforgiving random chaos.

One of the harshest realities of Perthro is the suggestion that the universe is ultimately meaningless -- a suggestion that taken too much to heart can drive us to madness and suicide. Many people are, at first, deeply disturbed or depressed by this idea, and will delude themselves by various degrees through fantasy that things have deeper meaning, even if we cannot understand it. The creation of meaning is actually necessary to our survival!

Properly examined, Perthro suggests that the fundamental background of the meaninglessness it represents is the equivalent of a blank canvas of infinite possibilities. It empowers us to consciously create ourselves and fulfill our human potential. It allows us to consciously evolve. The meaninglessness and nothingness only threaten us if we wish to shirk the responsibility of living our lives by choice, rather than by chance or by someone else's rules. We can even harness this creativity in shaping our destiny, making it easier to predict our future. In essence, the secret of Perthro is the secret of the runes -- to bring us past the need for divination and into the realm of transformation and manifestation.

The energy of this rune flows from the unmanifested into the manifest. Being born from non-being. It is random because it can represent events that have no cause, such as quantum events. These events, without causation and outside of the normal flow of reaction, transcend probabilities and are interwoven with the very fabric of our universe. Their consequences ensure a certain freedom within the system, and prevent a clockwork, deterministic universe from being possible. It is Perthro, ultimately, that insures the future is unwritten, and that the past can always be broken away from.

Algiz - "Elk"

KEY CONCEPTS: Protection, divinity, archetypes, higher self, mentors, protective teaching force, the divine plan, Valkyries, communication with the divine, evolution toward consciousness/godhood

Algiz is the ever alert guardian within us -- Our higher self, our higher awareness, that which is truly us. It protects us and serves us, even in our darkest days, even if we have ignored it a long time. It teaches us if we will listen. It waits for us to remember ourselves. It is the active protection and training of consciousness, rather than the inducement or simulation of conscious or transcendental experiences.

Algiz does not refer to an intoxicated state of divine inspiration. This is a misconception, and to experience this state is a consequence of imbalance. Algiz is the requirement of the divine path for sobriety, constant vigilance and clear-headed awareness. Rather than an escape from reality, Algiz represents the futility of over-dependence on such escapism. While the children play, and imagine, Algiz watches, teaches and protects.

I've always pictured Algiz as a satellite dish or antennae connecting us to our higher self. For me, a forward thinker of a digital age, that is the imagery that strongly resonates. While Ansuz remains the persuasive, inspired communication of the poet, the form of communication Algiz represents is with divine, intelligent beings, as we perceive them in the universe. Our higher self takes on many forms on our path to its discovery, always there to be listened to. One potent form in rune lore is that of the Valkyrie -- an image in which the later Angel image is rooted.

That we have such a higher self is a near inarguable certainty. All of us feel it, though we do not all feel it the same way. Some project it into the universe as a favored god, others merely as a desire to improve themselves. We are almost always painfully aware of our potential, even if it is forced silent into unconsciousness.

Our need to evolve, to transcend, to become one with our ideas of godhood is built into our every cell. It may be a consequence of the simple facts of natural selection and evolution, but the god-self archetype is very heavily ingrained in all of us.

It is possible to perceive the divine plan, that is, perceive the ways in which the universe acts that insures that life continues to progress, evolve, and transcend its current circumstances. Because it is possible to perceive this plan, it is possible to align oneself to it, to draw inspiration, teaching and power from it. This act of alignment is synonymous with the activation of one's higher self.

Algiz is the teacher-self teaching itself -- protecting itself and the unawakened -- and awakening on behalf of the yet to awaken. It is not judgemental of its students, nor does its interest necessarily lay in hastening the awakening of others. Awakening is a byproduct of its ultimate activities.

Algiz represents a super-consciousness that is above our current level of awareness, yet which is composed in part by our combined consciousness. It is at this level that our god-selves operate, and at this level that protection and counsel from those powers can be drawn from. It is this super-conscious level that is generally being referred to by our personal metaphor of a divine plan.

There are brief, intoxicating moments that the mind may suddenly rise to the level of the super-conscious. They rarely ever leave us the same afterward, and we can spend years recovering from what have seen. I say recovering, because we lose some of our stability in order to get ourselves moving. It is hard not to get carried away with the intoxication of being exposed to what feels like divine teachings.

However, Algiz represents the required surrender of that intoxicated state to a more stable, conscious, step-by-step rise into the super-consciousness of our higher self. Algiz helps us surrender our addiction to our personal self so that more of the higher self can take over. The teacher must become the teachings, practice what they preach and bring much more than a 'glimpse' of the divine into reality.

The proper alignment with the divine plan, the higher self and the protective teaching force of the universe comes by careful listening and adjusting. The sacred white elk, which is represented by Algiz, was revealed as a thing bordering on hallucination to the hunters who had spent several days in silence and solitude, tracking an invisible prey. The hunt required correct awareness.

Correct listening to the teaching voice of the universe is a difficult task. It is quite possible to be seen as insane, and in fact become insane, if one does not exercise the vigilant care of the watchful guardian aspect of Algiz. Other people may sometimes appear in the form of a mentor or teacher, but it is our higher self that is responsible, not the teacher, for their apparition -- and as a result the student who is loyal to his higher self is always destined to surpass any mortal teacher. The teachings manifest in many forms, not only the runes, and we are frequently tested and challenged to consider, even accept, other viewpoints. To the extent that we fail to do so, we are limited.

Our higher self is forgiving, if we are humble and genuine in our desire to learn from it. It holds no resentment or judgement. With infinite patience, Algiz represents our benevolent super-conscious teacher-self. It points to the basic fact that the universe is fundamentally good but also that this fundamental goodness and divinity is set apart and ultimately incomprehensible to the human mind. It is good despite us, even despite war and injustice -- it is ready to protect and teach, even in our darkest hours.

The energy of Algiz flows from the mundane and elevates time, space and self to the higher vibration of the sacred. This higher vibration then demands to be actualized *as* the mundane -- so that the divine plan is realized in everyday life.

Because it is so much a part of us, beyond our control, we cannot avoid trying to fulfill our inmost potential. It manifests strongly and becomes the sun (Sowilo) of our psychological universe, inimical to our attempts to shirk our responsibilities toward actualizing our god-self. The secret of Algiz is that you are never your higher self. There is always a yet-higher self. This is the key to its ancient power.

Sowilo - "Sun"

KEY CONCEPTS: guidance, goal setting, success, motivation, life-giving force, action, the sun, the star sol, the daystar

Sowilo means sun, specifically our sun -- Sól or Sunna (both are Old Norse). There have been thinkers who have known that the sun was a star at least since Anaxagoras, who lived in Athens, Greece, around 450 BC. It is quite likely that learned sages among many cultures figured this out even earlier. The idea was held at bay by the Church for over a thousand years and those who taught of it were punished.

Metaphysically, Sowilo represents both the outer sun, and the inner sun or seat of the soul. When we master the energy of Sowilo, the warmth and clarity that radiates from us naturally falls upon everyone and everything we touch. It is a deeply ordering energy and, properly understood, it is a rune of healing and wholeness. Sowilo's power lies in forever strengthening the energy centers of the body.

Sowilo is the transmutation of thought into energy for action. It represents a forward looking aspect of our consciousness and supplies the fuel that burns within us to motivate ourselves to change. When we adopt a goal, our lives begin to fall into orbit around it -- Sowilo speaks of the conscious selection and magic of goals. Our ability to identify courses of action through thought and transmute our ideas into a real change is the key to maintaining the wholeness that Sowilo points to.

The sun is an unimaginable nuclear furnace, as are all stars, but only a trickle of that energy reaches our world. Life uses that energy very efficiently. It doesn't take massive energy to do what we need to do. We must guide ourselves, or accept guidance, which allows us to break things down and accomplish small victories. These become larger victories incrementally. In using Sowilo magic, small, incremental steps are taken. Certain things are added and certain things removed from our complex system in order to maintain a healthy equilibrium.

The secret Sowilo reveals is very much a one step after the other process. Health is maintained through many small decisions. Wealth is generated through an army of tiny habits. As a whole, this army of action adds up to something large and powerful, however this is, after a sense, an illusion. Each factor is incorporated individually into the totality of action, when it is most appropriate to do so. We know which small things to change as they arise, because our behavior orbits around a conscious goal, just as the Earth around the sun, day by day, season after season.

While Algiz points toward the teachings of the divine and the higher self, Sowilo is the rune of a thousand implementations, adjusting our reality and our habits on a daily basis, in small ways, according to the truths we have uncovered and learned. It is the difference between knowing and doing.

This is the basic power of non-destructive fire, or combustion. The energy is very similar to the metabolic energy that keeps our bodies warm efficiently. This is also why Sowilo is linked to health and wholeness. Our being is actually the sum of billions upon billions of tiny processes that developed over countless millennia.

Efficiency means consuming as little energy as possible for the maximum result. Therefore Sowilo teaches us to unite clarity of thought (sunlight) with gradual self-perfection (evolution). The perfection of this principle is intrinsic to the life of the truly wise who would take their fates into their own hands.

Unlike many of the other runes of the second Aett, Sowilo seems more benevolent and supportive to our human situation, creating a polarity with Hagalaz on the other end of the row. However, it acts just as indifferently -- the sun shines on the good and the wicked alike. Just as many small changes can consciously be made, inattentiveness to the principles Sowilo points to will allow thousands of unconscious factors to cause instability, chaos or even our inevitable destruction. It is a secret available to anyone, even those who would use it for great evil -- such as Nazi Germany's S.S. in the mid-twentieth century. Be wary of letting a small evil in the door, for greater ones will inevitably follow.

Sowilo is a counter-point to Hagalaz in this Aett. Sowilo functions incrementally, whereas the energy of Hagalaz can furiously undo much of its work in an instant. Yet they are remarkably balanced -- a polarity worth noting and contemplating when looking at this row as a whole.

THE THIRD AETT

The Third Aett, as a row, is concerned with the evolutionary laws of the universe. The runes of this row are sequenced according to a sovereign order, beginning with the most fundamental and basic cosmic laws (such as gravity) through to the laws of enlightened consciousness and heaven on earth. Each rune represents a distinct principle which orders action in the universe. Through these runes we see our own connection and inseparableness from the universe as well as the inevitability of evolution and awakening.

Tiwaz - "The god, Tyr"

KEY CONCEPTS: balance, justice, rationality, sacrifice for the greater good, righteousness, sovereign order, right decision making

Tiwaz represents the fundamental cosmic law. In Norse mythology, Tyr, despite being a god of justice and honor, tricks the Fenris wolf in order to prevent it from devouring the world. The Fenris wolf could be seen as a massive black hole, growing relentlessly to consume all creation. The god Tyr, sacrificed his right hand to implement the balancing laws of the physical universe. The cosmos is thus maintained through the laws of physics, not the hand of a god. The story of Tyr and the Fenris wolf can be seen as a metaphor for understanding that fact.

This basic cosmic law establishes a sovereign order in the universe which allows evolution to occur through structural laws (Newtonian), relativity (Einstein) and inherent freedom (Quantum probabilities). In such conditions, it is inevitable that more complex realities gradually and exponentially emerge, such as galaxies which form nebulae, which form stars, which form planets, some of which form life, from which consciousness sometimes emerges, and so on, to yet unknown consequences.

Because there are fundamental laws like this to the universe, the universe is essentially just. Human cultures, and individuals in them, may have different opinions of what is fair and just, but the cosmic law comes prior to human drama, indeed long before human existence.

Knowledge of and alignment to the cosmic laws of Tiwaz is really an alignment to reality, no matter how harsh or unfair we believe it to be. It must conform to particular laws, rules and probabilities because of the truth Tiwaz represents. This is a very powerful realization, an affirming act. Although indifferent to our traditional notions of justice, the cosmic law is consistent, fair and therefore ultimately good. Gravity keeps us from floating off the planet, but if you decide to jump off a cliff, it isn't as if the law of gravity is going to make an exception for you -- it is in this way that gravity could be seen as "fair".

Tiwaz also points to the fairness that reality is accessible to every person, though it is not always easy for the human mind to stick to the evidence and the facts. In Tiwaz's form of justice, ignorance of the law is no excuse - the world doesn't stop turning on account of any individual concern, nor does it conform to one's particular beliefs or expectations.

Tiwaz often seems to ask us to stand up for what is true, and sacrifice our wishes and fantasies in order to embrace reality -- even if it is a harsh one. How can we serve this ultimate understanding of justice, bring it into the human realm, and into our ethics and morality, if we cannot come to terms with the way things truly are?

Universal laws, rules, facts and evidence are the basics of this rune, and indeed justice. Rational explanation, balanced and unbiased argument, investigation and research, respect and honor for truth -- all of these are powerful keys to unlocking the secrets of universal justice and the eternal cosmic order. Tiwaz is also a rune of navigation, plainly symbolized by the arrow pointing forward, upward, north; an excellent symbol for our inner moral compass.

As Sowilo represents the star Sól, Tiwaz points toward the north star, Polaris. More generally, Tiwaz represents the vast array of stars and galaxies which make up the navigable night sky, stretching on infinitely, but sharing the cosmic laws between them. By studying them we learned to navigate the seas, and with astrology even believed ourselves capable of navigating our fates. Someday, we may navigate the void between the stars themselves. Like the stars, shining in vast darkness, Tiwaz gives us the strength for the 'good fight', the energy to shine in the darkest of days here on Earth and perhaps protect and guide others who cannot defend themselves.

If we identify and follow the permanent and unchanging laws of our universe, we can navigate it successfully, and make the right decisions. Respecting and understanding the cosmic laws confers a power only feebly mimicked by the lawyers, judges and politicians of human societies. Failing to honor justice, the individual comes to pointless ruin, and a society that tolerates injustice is indeed an unhappy and backwards one. Yet a single star in the night sky would still be seen to shine across the land. So do we shine when we live justly every day.

Berkano - "Birch Goddess"

KEY CONCEPTS: Birth, abiogenesis/ biopoesis, rebirth, regrowth, regeneration, silence, plantlife, emergence, sanctuary

Berkano is the rune of life's emergence from the fundamental cosmic law. In natural science, abiogenesis or biopoesis is the study of how biological life arises from inorganic matter, that is -- the method by which life on Earth arose. The Berkano rune then, points to this biopoesis wherever it occurs in the universe, and its particular qualities of reproduction, regeneration and adaptation to the rhythms of varied environments. An example of one such event, to which the rune refers, is life's spring-time renewal from the cold of winter.

This rune points to the laws that govern the life force, itself. Berkano is the "mindless intelligence", where it becomes clear that we are dealing with animated life rather than inert substance. Berkano represents the point at which the complexity of reactions becomes high enough for basic intelligence to emerge, and at a more abstract level, any sort of emergence from the previous constraints of a living system.

Science argues against what some call "intelligent design" -- that there is some sort of designer required other than the initial cosmic laws (Tiwaz). The life force and its proto-intelligence emerges from the inevitable escalation of complexity in the universe. This realization makes it difficult to imagine that we are the only planet with life on it, or that carbon-based life is the only type of living thing that can emerge from the complexity of the cosmos, or that human consciousness the only consciousness possible.

All this talk of complexity runs counter to the feeling of Berkano, which is that of patience, simplicity and motherliness. The energy of Berkano is that of the womb, the metabolism and the immune system. It is the point of contact between life and non-life in nature, and how life integrates seamlessly with its environment. When we talk of Berkano we are talking about a very simple, straight forward intelligence, regardless of how it astounds the human mind. The rules that the essential life force follows lay the ground work for further complexity and intelligence to emerge.

We can see how bacteria and plant-life, represented as a totality by the Birch Goddess, signify a major shift in the norm of cosmic law set forth in Tiwaz. They compose, by far, most of the life on Earth, and occupy much more of the evolutionary time line and it is this bulk and extensiveness that impregnates the Berkano rune with meaning.

Berkano is able to draw its energy from light and heat -- both of which have a profound affect on the human psyche. By exploring Berkano, we tap into the qualities that make life fundamentally immortal, the basics of reproduction and regeneration on a cellular level. Our body is an awesome product of this patient intelligence -- growing system on top of system on top of system for billions of years. Each system nurtures and supports the next just as a mother and child. In this sense we get a strong impression that there is a Mother Earth, or Gaia.

The tendency of life to heal itself, adapt to what it cannot heal, or construct niches in which its environment no longer harms it, is implicit to the life force Berkano represents. It displays a tendency for life to care about itself and provide sanctuary for itself.

At the level of 'All Life In the Universe', the differences between species, between what is plant, mammal, amphibian, bacterium, etc. is irrelevant. From our perspective, there is conflict, but from the perspective of this "mindless intelligence" that is the life force, it has the single aim of creating more life, copying itself and growing and regrowing in any way, shape or form possible. The emphasis on copying can be seen in the shape of the rune itself.

If we look at the murk-stave qualities of the rune, and reverse its meanings, we could easily come to the conclusion that Berkano could signify parasitism, viral infection, and disease -- unfortunate anomalies that piggy-back on the life force's own fundamental nature. Berkano does not discriminate in its love for all life, and represents the full spectrum of its consequences. This is quite inhuman to us, and we often run up against the hardship and suffering caused by disease, and the burden of the parasitic phenomenon is mirrored at every level of life.

Berkano's ultimately mindless care and indiscriminate patience and love for this task is staggeringly powerful, and we may someday discover that it unites the stars in a way we find inconceivable today. Our human minds reel in face of its beauty and through Berkano we can access the basic love inherent in the cosmic law. But this love is far more vast than human love, and therefor not always possible for us to understand.

The secret of Berkano is simplicity, attentiveness and care for details. It is the process of perfecting a labor of love -- and seems to be at the heart of all life.

Ehwaz - "Horse"

KEY CONCEPTS: trust, teamwork, emotion, sexuality, instinct, animals, friendship, love, anima/animus, inner-harmony, partnership

The horse and rider exemplify this rune, because of a particular and special bond they signify. The horse, as with many animals, is emotion based. When we unite human consciousness with this animal emotion, whether in the form of a partner or our own internal emotional core, we are empowered and united as one. This is also a powerful secret in mastering our emotions to reduce impulsiveness and reactive unconscious behavior.

Ehwaz is a rune of trust, teamwork and love. It involves wisely and intelligently nurturing a relationship over time, building and maintaining trust, and sharpening sensitivity to one's own emotions and those of others. This is all essential work in understanding and working with the energy of Ehwaz.

This rune signifies the arising of emotion from the unconscious life force, pointing backward to the evolution of mammals, but also beyond to instinct -- which is really just a form of emotion that happens faster, in reflexes and impulses that we haven't consciously mastered.

Despite our having evolved into what we are now, emotion still exists as a chemical basis for many of our habitual thought patterns and archetypes. We are much more connected to this past than most of us care to acknowledge. Emotion is so powerful that much of what we believe is rational thinking is actually backward rationalization -- thoughts that justify, explain and abstract emotions that may otherwise be difficult for us to handle.

Ehwaz also represents our emotional projections. When we deny our emotions, they do not go away, but warp into forms we more easily deal with. This is closely tied with the reality of archetypes. Projections seem real, and often seem as if they are qualities that exist in others, or in the world at large. But our feelings do not exist 'out there' of course. They are within. Our own minds often unconsciously confuse something we feel in our body for something in the world 'causing' us to feel that way. This happens because our animal mind is at odds with the later developed human mind, and we get conflicting messages.

Through emotional work and the correction of our conditioned thought patterns, we can 'tame' our reactive animal nature and elevate it to a powerful partner alongside our more rational will, just like that horse and rider which Ehwaz represents. But it is an ongoing partnership, a constant give and take, requiring sensitivity, vigilance and excellent timing.

In the inner world, the energy of Ehwaz is used to form a bond of friendship with oneself. We often beat ourselves up, and say negative things to ourself, think ill of our actions and are unable to forgive our past or believe in ourselves. There is a lot of self-inflicted emotional abuse. Ehwaz reveals that there is nothing standing in our way of being friendly when dealing with ourself. It is perhaps among the greatest transmutation of one's life when the inner world begins to calm itself and become friendly and self-supportive. This is the ultimate meaning of the horse and rider, of the taming of our wild, hostile emotional animal side and its subsequent transformation into a powerful and sympathetic ally. We must offer ourselves unconditional love and acceptance, like a horse offers to its rider.

What is most important to this is the realization that we must co-operate and compromise with ourselves. Also key is to know that we cannot help but have emotions, and we cannot help but construct thoughts to rationalize them -- this happens automatically. However we can train our thoughts and emotions to present themselves more clearly, and we can learn to master and direct them, rather than be constantly at their mercy.

Partnerships with other humans also arise from this rune, and the emotional bonds that form are primarily what is referred to. Ehwaz shows us that positive bonds develop through teamwork. Listening and empathy are the major tools of Ehwaz and are at the core of strengthening relationships.

With humans, Ehwaz includes the realm of loving relationship, marriage and sexuality. When we seek a life partner, we tap deeply into the energies and teachings of this rune. The sensitivity, understanding and commitment required for two beings to love one another and enhance one another's life in a healthy way is learned first here.

In our inner world, Ehwaz represents the Fetch, or what Carl Jung called the anima (or animus). This is always of the opposite gender

THE BOOK OF RUNE SECRETS

-- not necessarily the physical gender but the psychological one. It is the relationship we have with what has been unmanifest in us, and we feel it strongly as a lack until we come to terms with it.

The outward expression of this realization happened in human history when we began to see that we could live alongside various other intelligent species, such as dogs, horses, cats and birds. The ancients also often had spirit animals that represented the fact that our emotional animal self was still very integrated into the totality of our being.

Music has a definite role to play in the makeup of the rune Ehwaz, and shares many fundamental similarities in its structure to the process of building trust, cultivating dependability or predictability, and violating that predictability in a way that keeps things playful and fresh. Each of a horse's gaits has a particular rhythm, and along with the sound of our heartbeat, has an archetypal influence on all music.

The energy of this rune flows in reciprocal feedback between increasingly cooperative beings, strengthening itself and growing towards higher patterns of love.

Mannaz - "Humankind"

KEY CONCEPTS: humankind, intelligence, mind and memory, thought, imagination, human evolution, divine structure in human civilization, analysis, planning, collaboration, self in service of community, the human condition

Mannaz represents human individuality and co-operative self-actualization, harmony within the community and within the context of the collective. It is the rune of the human intellect, its consequences, and the cosmic laws by which both are governed. This rune points to the realm of thought, its processes and the human behaviors that arise as a result.

When we thoroughly understand our own human nature, we begin to understand the collective human condition. This is due to an understanding that everyone is human, and that although uniqueness and differences are real, there is an underlying structure to all behavior that every human generally has in common. Awakening to this secret is not easily attained, because it requires a lifetime of contemplation. But it is a very worthy pursuit!

Through understanding Mannaz, our shrouded human origins are also revealed. Our lack of memory at birth and through very early childhood is mirrored in the birth and early childhood of humankind. The conditions under which humankind first evolved have profound psychological influence, just as our own individual early development has had on us, even though we cannot recall it.

Discoveries about our early conditions can tell us about ourselves, and equally, discoveries about ourselves can tell us about our early conditions -- at least in a mythical way. This narrative, a mix of memory and imagination, has always been fundamental to how our mind works with time, and our brain makes little distinction between what it remembers and what it has vividly imagined. This is the basis of Jungian psychoanalysis.

Mannaz is the rune of human intelligence and the rational mind. Our power to master ourselves and co-create our environment lay locked in the mystery of Mannaz -- but it is a mystery that does not so easily surrender itself. It is too easy to assume we are using the energy of Mannaz correctly, when in fact we are not.

Mannaz represents the realization of the significant ways in which humankind differs from all other known life on Earth, particularly due to our intelligence, our memory, our analytical abilities and our emerging roles as co-creators alongside what we once understood as gods and nature.

Mannaz departs from the self-actualization of Algiz and Sowilo because it is an integrative rune that defers to its understanding of the collective reality. The energy of Mannaz expands our awareness beyond ourselves and into the structures which all of our individual relationships form on a super-social level. Rather than accessing our intuition or the subliminal, the secret of this rune allows us to access the superliminal: that which is above the scope of our normal awareness to perceive.

At the level of the superliminal, our individual minds combine to create the cosmic laws of collective intelligence. Embracing the secrets of Mannaz, we often outgrow and forget about ourselves as our interests align with the intelligence beyond.

Socially, Mannaz represents the tendency of humans to organize into larger structures, and for society to increase in complexity while the individuals within it form progressively diverse roles for themselves and relationships with one another. We have an astounding flexibility as a species, due to our creativity, and there have been thousands of cultures with unique traditions and successful ways of organizing and viewing the world. Accessing the secret that Mannaz points toward, we create the opportunity to appreciate all of these expressions of the human mind in society, without prejudice.

Mannaz unlocks the human horizon, and signifies the point at which the universe has begun to become aware of itself, through us. Through this emerging awareness it becomes an active creator of itself. We are inseparable from the universe and therefore, when we observe the universe, it is the universe itself observing.

Until recently, we have anthropomorphized the universe into concepts such as gods, or abstracted it as "nature" by projecting our own image into the world around us. This is no longer necessary, and a great awakening and evolutionary leap is possible, if we embrace it. The ancients claimed our ancestry descended from the gods only to prophesize our re-ascent.

The major consequence of tapping into Mannaz' energy is that the future opens up to us. No other animal has such powers of long-range prediction, strategy nor ability to influence future events. When we as a civilization learn to harness the potential inherent in Mannaz, we open the door to a sustainable planetary civilization, and can inevitably bridge the gap between the stars.

So the individual changes that Mannaz invokes are mirrored by humankind's collective wish to actualize its own potential. This is the major insight from looking into Mannaz. Once reached, in whatever form, this insight powers the mind to dedicate itself to consciously improving the collective condition.

Mannaz, embraced, utterly transmutes fear of the unknown into an awareness of its potentialities. In this way, it consciously activates the human imagination -- which is the ultimate expression of our divinity.

However, Mannaz is but one rune, demonstrating that we hold no central, definitive place in the cosmos, it dooms us to have little individual power over the collective current. This, in effect could be its murk-stave -- the helplessness of the individual to impact collective intelligence. We feel this most often when we adopt the mistaken idea that the masses are incompetent fools. Believing yourself to be more intelligent than the collective is an obstacle on the path to harnessing the powers that Mannaz represents. It is a principle inclusive of others, their abilities and their perspectives.

When we reverse Mannaz, we in every way see the negative impact of individual vices and how they influence the whole toward dysfunction. We may even see its ultimate perversion as the megalomanic: one obsessed with and driven by personal ego, never satisfied or respectful of due process, projecting power over the human order with destructive consequences.

Laguz - "Water"

KEY CONCEPTS: the unconscious, unity of all life, biosphere, imagination, psychic power, dreams, karma, projection, collective memory, archetypal patterning, depth, flow of reality

Laguz means water, which is a symbol of unconscious and invisible life currents, unity, flow and formlessness. It is the psychic landscape of all life, that which transcends thought and integrates mind into being.

Water is the ancient mirror -- the first surface the evolving ego likely had to identify itself was the calm surface of standing water. But a surface identity of associated concepts, an "I" or "Me" that is a reality of our lives, is the domain of Isa. Laguz is concerned with activity happening deeper within the self, through the self, into the deep unconscious -- that which we essentially are, but are unaware of being.

The substance of Laguz is everywhere present, pervades all things and underlies all manifestation. It is the living energy of which everything bases itself. Most of the Earth's surface is covered in water -- it is the dominant feature of this living planet, making it an apt metaphor.

All life is dependent on water, and water makes up most of our physical composition. Our water however, is part of a unified system -- we drink, perspire, expel and recycle, as do all other beings, transmuting liquids and materials into various forms, which are in turn used by other creatures or transformed by natural processes. This creates an ecological biosphere, of which we are but one small part.

Notice that this fact underpins some spiritual notions such as wyrd (or karma). Our actions, no matter how small, circulate the entire system, but unconsciously, blindly. We rarely see their results directly. By tapping into the secrets of Lagaz we can get a deeper understanding, however, of how these actions work.

At the level of the biosphere is our conception of Gaia, or Mother Earth. Most cultures and spiritual traditions have a deep feeling for this, and orient much of their collective wisdom around what we can learn of the biosphere. Laguz, that is, water, is the most important chemical compound in the biosphere, thus also represents this shared unity.

All life on the entire earth can be seen as a living being, with it's own super-consciousness. This consciousness is not human, but includes the human, and all human activity, seamlessly within it. It is the cosmic law that we are inseparable from all other things, whether we understand those things as living, inanimate, or the laws of the universe themselves.

Where Isa can symbolize form, Laguz points toward the formless. It reveals the ultimate paradox, that there is no nature, no true equilibrium, no invisible hand. Nature can take on radically new forms because there are no fixed forms in the universe. Everything is constantly changing, and that constant change creates a reactive matrix which flows with infinite complexity into and through all things.

This selfsame formlessness, this shape-shifting, creates the flow of immortality. It demonstrates that our birth and our death are arbitrary human markers, and that in a very real way, we are composed of the 'stuff of life', and simply disperse back into that general flow on occasion of our deaths. Nothing essential is ever created or lost, from the perspective of Laguz. We are one with all form, yet we are formless as our essential being. Harnessing the power of Laguz is akin learning to let go of one's temporary form and perceive oneself as a seamless flow, permanently united with the universe.

Laguz teaches us to look into the depth and darkness of our unconscious, and to see in the universe our 'reflection', to know when what we see is actually our own shadow, or image impersonating reality. Proper discovery and use of the way in which our own mind projects itself into the outer world is a fantastic way of looking back at ourselves. We often attribute to the universe qualities that aren't really there, but emerge because of some unexamined contradiction or conflict within ourselves. We see our own reflection in many things, and if we become conscious of this, we learn of ourselves as if holding ourselves up to a mirror.

Dreams are what happen when we shut our senses down and only our reflection, in the form of memory, imagination, unconscious narrative and patterning is active. We still dream while awake, but it is masked by its seamless integration with our sensory-based perception. The study of our dreams is useful for both filtering out unwanted projection in our day to day life, or identifying things happening within our waking lives that may be wise to pay attention to. However, dream interpretation is a difficult task -- each dream uses unique, private symbols and images that you must learn to decode for yourself.

Within the collective unconscious represented by Laguz, we find certain loose forms that life has repeated over and over in its 3.5 billion year journey. These are called archetypes, and we often access archetypes unconsciously, because a person or a situation fits or flows into them easily. This is also the origin of intuition, and of the underlying patterns that our personal stories often seem to loosely follow. Archetypes often play heavily in our dreams, as well. They are our common experience, and they are built into the fabric of our being by eons of repetition. The runes, as I explain them, represent many of these archetypes.

Because of all this, Laguz hints at a realm of intelligence beyond our powers of regular thought and analysis. It represents the stillness and formlessness of the awareness inherent in every cell in all life. This intelligence is universal and vast. We experience it because of our connection to all the subtle unconscious processes we are invisibly, but physically linked to. It is the simple, silent listening consciousness.

Laguz teaches that if we become very still and clear ourselves of the turbulence of emotions and thoughts, we can tap into this simple, silent listening state and find connection and great insight there, a sharpening of senses which exposes the waking dream. It is as if we reach the ocean of the unconscious and can see ourselves reflected more clearly within it, and therefore learn what we truly are by filtering out surface appearances.

Inguz - "Seed"

KEY CONCEPTS: replication, creation, conscious generation, inner-child, the core pattern + algorithms (eg. DNA), wholeness, symmetry, planned bursts, isolation, incubation, gestation

Inguz represents a simple, but complex idea -- that of the seed. Inguz points toward the cosmic law that governs the essential creativity inherent to the fabric of existence.

Inguz is that part of life which implicitly copies, varies and selects in order to produce, in the most simple way possible, infinite and awesome complexity. Inguz represents real algorithms that nature constructs to allow life itself to spread and evolve. The seed is also known in science as DNA. In it's psychic form, it is known as an 'idea' or a meme. Ideas are the mind's mirroring of this same cosmic law that governs the seed found also in our genetic makeup. The seed's penultimate purpose is to pass itself on. But its ultimate secret is much more extensive.

Inguz, or 'Ing', is in our language today. We use 'ing' when we speak of 'doing', as in 'sitting' or 'running' or 'thinking', which are active processes, not objects. In our language we are object-centric. We focus on the noun. Adopting the secrets of Inguz allows us to become process-centric, so that we may see the world and Life as verbs.

With regards to the generation of ideas, there are always many ways in which someone may be 'thinking', and the process is not always the same, but there is some sort of process occurring. No thought exists in isolation and no creation is fully original.

Inguz is the very process by which creation occurs, including the incubation and gestation of the seed, its germination and subsequent development and growth. When the process has come to a peak, the being generated by the seed in turn actively produces new seeds, which vary but are basically the same. Over time, this process has radical impacts on the chaotic system of nature, and amazing variation emerges, new complexity, new forms and new modes of creation. Even new modes of being, new cosmic laws and entire universes.

In human consciousness, the ability to reproduce symbols which represented ideas was an unprecedented leap in evolution, and has led to our rapid rise as the dominant species on earth. An idea follows many of the same patterns an organism does, and in this way, the principle underlying Inguz can be understood in astounding depth.

Harnessing the energy of Inguz for our purposes requires that we become conscious of the ways in which a small seed can be planted in the right environment, or nurtured, into a powerful new mode of being. We open up room for Inguz energy through the deliberate act of creating time and space for ourselves and for the people and events we wish to affect.

Creation using Inguz includes the conscious manifestation of such seeds, often in the form of ideas that are then made into reality through a 'psychic agriculture' which entails working smarter, not harder. But an elegant enough seed, once condensed, works its magic by itself -- it is so simple, so condensed but so complete, that as it unfolds it follows an unstoppable pattern. The seed begins mirroring the cosmic law by defining its own rules and limits even further as it grows. We can barely imagine sometimes how a tree emerges from a simple acorn, how a forest emerges from a single tree, and how that forest creates a new environment where other seeds and beings thrive as well.

Creation of the seed looks like an act of diminishment, but it is unimaginably powerful. Think of the tiniest atom, and of the power released when it is tampered with. Small, precise actions can have vast consequences -- and if our attention to detail allows us to penetrate the mysteries of the very tiny, we can affect the very large. It is interesting to think of the potential paradox that by doing nothing, one accomplishes everything.

So, Inguz unlocks the energy of continuation and generation but also the magic of discovering the very essence of a thing, the simple algorithm that will most ensure its spread and growth into the universe. It is the cosmic law of the infinitesimally small and its symmetry with the infinitely large.

In this way, Inguz is a rune of wholeness. When we summon up Inguz as energy and understand its teachings, it signals the integration of the four selves -- physical, emotional, mental and spiritual -- into one centered being. This being is our eternal child self, our inmost vitality and the acknowledgement that ultimate completion is not only impossible, but undesirable. It is the being most aligned with rampant creativity and originality, and the ultimate source of all we consider genius.

Dagaz - "Day"

KEY CONCEPTS: Hyper-consciousness, awakening, conceptual realization, enlightenment, non-duality, synthesis, transmutation, awareness, paradigm shift, faith

Dagaz is the sunrise of consciousness, that hazy moment where out of the night emerges the light of day. A new reality dawns on us and we are refreshed, infused with rested energy and excitement for the day ahead.

Dagaz symbolizes the ordinariness of the fully conscious state -- that the aim is not to transcend reality by becoming conscious, but by letting consciousness shine upon reality with the force of daybreak.

This rune of spiritual awakening points also towards the tendency for consciousness to emerge in the universe as the cosmic law unfolds. It is the inevitability of awakening, the promise of sunrise. It is infused with the inspiration of hope, because from the very first tiny movements that begun life on this planet, the sun, once set, has risen once again from the darkness.

Dagaz also signifies a deep shift in perspective that is truly powerful and important, if we can realize it within ourselves. Just as it is the Earth turning, not the sun moving, that causes the illusion of sunrise and sunset, so too does our conscious awareness orbit a greater consciousness. Although night and day have profound and undeniable effects on daily life, ultimately, it is not the sun that moves in relation to Earth. Can you see that, as you watch the sun climb into the sky? Can you see that the sun is outside of what we routinely assume is 'time'?

Can you see that your conscious awareness is but a single perspective, connected to its own rhythms and cycles, one satellite amongst many which orbit the greater consciousness inherent in all life, in all spaces and times?

Dagaz is the final synthesis of paradox, the final disappearance of ego in the form of self and other, and the dissolution of opposites. It is a power of consciousness which emerges and unfolds in the universe. The cosmic law directs our flow towards it. It is outside of time; it began before there was such a thing as beginnings, and it exists at the end of infinity.

Time was created out of the big bang, therefore the big bang did not 'happen' but IS happening. Quantum science has shown that not all events have causes. Chaos theory shows that strange attractors emerge from basic rules, that rules can change due to circumstances that previous rules created, with a phenomenon called emergence.

All this tells us a story of a universe that defies our human understanding in tremendous ways, and yet it is possible to understand and appreciate, because it is built into our very structure. Indeed, we are fashioned from the sun -- every atom, every molecule, forged in the furnace of sun after sun after sun.

The secret of Dagaz is that we are powerful beyond measure -- and all this is so ordinary and everyday that we take it completely for granted. It is invisible to us. Light allows us to see all things -- yet we do not see light itself! This kind of paradoxical synthesis of extremes is inherent to any talk of Dagaz.

Dagaz energy spends itself freely and purposelessly. Dagaz is the transcendence of time. It takes its time being timeless. It enjoys the moment and the fundamental goodness of all things. It is above our short term moral judgements as human beings, like all other cosmic law.

Dagaz is the energy that the universe spends being playful -- an intense playfulness that is generally beyond our mortal understanding, and yet, when struck with the illumination of Dagaz, we cannot help but experience it as true, even join in. It is precisely the energy we feel on a warm day, outdoors, free from all worry, with nothing but time on our hands.

Its symbolism reveals to us that the universe is ultimately indivisible: there is no rune in the Elder Futhark for night, nor the glow of the moon, nor darkness amongst its symbols -- those things are understood to be absences and reflections and nothings, rather than things in and of themselves.

Polarities and paradoxes seem like profound riddles to our minds, and we love to contemplate the mystery, bask in it, wonder, explore, invent and play. It is no coincidence that our minds developed in this way. This love and playfulness is inherent in the cosmic law, and represents the penultimate human experience --

the inevitable awakening, the sunrise that makes us feel a golden age is calling to us from just over the horizon. Enlightenment.

Using the magic of Dagaz, we can transmute ourselves powerfully into increasingly awakened beings, shedding all confusion in favor of clarity. The greater consciousness that this rune secretly points to is everywhere, all the time, present but not perceived. It is like the light of day -- the lightening of sky on the horizon.

Othala - "Homeland"

KEY CONCEPTS: ancestral spiritual power, inheritance, heaven on earth, paradise, utopia, estate, freedom from worldly possessions

Othala signals the final and eternal beauty of 'heaven' in the image of Asgard, and the love for one's home. It refers to a transcendence of geography, both planetary and cosmic. It is the individual, family or collective who have transcended culture, become a-cultural and fully human. Ideas of nationality, of tribe or clan, are no longer required. Cultural icons, symbols and languages become interchangeable as the root of all culture is opened within the mind of each person. One is at home everywhere. We are simply the human tribe.

This rune signifies Earth as the inherited homeland of all Earthlings, and thus our responsibilities to it, and to the future. This is the final rune, in my opinion, because it refers implicitly to our legacy, and what we leave behind as the inheritance of future generations. It places responsibility squarely in our hands and reminds us that we can take nothing with us past the gates of our own oblivion. It is the cosmic law that condemns any action (or inaction) which borrows or steals from the future as fundamentally insane. It demonstrates, as clear as mathematics, the foolishness of nationalism, violence and environmental destruction.

The energy of this rune, properly used, will reveal to the seeker how global unity can be peacefully achieved, without mass violence. Infamously misused and manifest as murk-stave by the Nazis, it contains an ancient, secret prophecy from the dawn of human civilization: that of one world, peacefully standing united and free.

Othala also represents the inherent nobility of those who honestly and humbly dedicate themselves to the continuation of their ancestral spiritual duty to use all of one's resources, wit and wisdom for the benefit of all Life, to generate true wealth and health in all realms, and to pass everything forward to future generations. Othala does not borrow from future generations, and instead seeks way to make Life sustainable, and the universe richer, for all. Poverty and greed are deeply intolerable to the true noble soul.

To be noble is to act noble -- it requires no riches, only virtue. Its wealth is generated for the benefit of all, and passed on selflessly to the future. This too is a lesson of Othala. This is true inheritance.

Othala's core power is the wise management of resources. In its magic, it draws on each rune's energy, where appropriate. It is most strongly realized and powerful when each rune is understood as equally important, and are activated with profound wisdom and care.

Othala links us to our ancestral heritage, to the very first humans who became conscious, began to think and seek something greater than a mere 'animal' existence. It harkens back to the day visionaries first developed the need to leave something behind for those that would come to be. These immortal visionaries have passed on to us an inheritance that we may all activate if we so chose, and that is to become immortal visionaries ourselves, to join the One Family, whose bond is greater than blood or breath, whose love for one another transcends space and time, even the unknown abyss.

These immortals are the warriors and protectors of consciousness, who are accepted into Valhalla and return to human existence again and again. Their numbers grow through the generations and Asgard, which represents the cosmic dominion of consciousness, expands toward the infinite.

Those who swear fealty to the energy of Othala come to know that working toward heaven on earth is heaven on earth. This rune's vision of a united world is an inevitable impetus because of the power of ordinary, every day, peaceful people interacting together in a mundane way, profound in its simplicity.

Where Life goes from there, the runes do not say, for the runes were made by humans for humans... and though humanity should not be underestimated, evolution will not stop with us. Far into the future, we will be something else entirely. It will not be the gods who shape us, but ourselves.

Afterword

Moving Beyond the Runes

The Elder Futhark runes are like a coded message sent to us from across the forgotten centuries. It is a time capsule in symbols. It is as if we sent it to ourselves, so that we could understand the unity of time. Just as our ancestors sent us this amazing message, 24 symbols long, we must in turn send a message to those who will someday call us their ancestors.

This will require embracing science and truth, probing our depths, helping one another learn, and exploring our contemporary cosmology in a way we have hitherto never believed possible. But we must believe. Those yet unborn people will be here long after we are gone, and for better or for worse will inherit every detail of the legacy we create.

Human knowledge is becoming both freely shareable and endlessly modifiable. The maximum amount of people will be called upon to participate in its generation, each according to their ability. This information will be produced for its use value, not for any exchange value, and the results of its use will be shared with the commons, which begins the cycle again, creating an exponential wealth of culture and lore.

I see this all the time in the technological sphere as a fundamental truth of emerging technologies. But it has, in effect, been the truth all along. What is occurring, really, is a growing awareness that we are in control. It will not be long before it profoundly affects the way in which human consciousness explores its own spirit.

Before this paradigm shift, new age thinking, as a branch of post-modernism, declared that there could be no consensus on reality, that all viewpoints were equally valid, that there could be no ultimate truth.

We now see that the ultimate truth is within. We are creators, that is a fact. Outward reality is created. It is a blank canvas. This is its truth. There is no individual viewpoint of it because it is not created by consensus, but by collaboration.

We have been creating our human reality unconsciously -- aware we have the potential to shape it but unaware of our innate responsibility to consciously do so.

Why can there be no consensus on reality? It is not because there is 'no one objective truth'. It is because the objective truth is that our brains have evolved to the point where reality is literally ours to create, and that it is perfectly proper to do so. In the case of the runes, we may not ever know exactly how the Germanic people, or the Norse, treated these symbols. But we can be assured they created their meaning and their magic. Why can we not do exactly as they did?

If I have conveyed anything to you, let it be this: it may not be the path of least resistance, and there may be a few laws of physics that frame our activities, but the obstacles you face in realizing your potential are ultimately self imposed illusions.

To be spiritual now, in the 21st century, means you cannot just read or worship a spiritual text and let someone else do your thinking and imagining.

You must create your own spiritual texts. Not only that, you must write them honestly and live them. You won't be teaching it to others either, you'll be teaching them to do as you did, but for themselves.

It is in your hands now. You must be that saviour, that guru, that mystic or sage which the future generations can benefit from. A future-wisdom rather than an ancient one. When we are the ancients ... what will be left, spiritually, of our culture?

We can no longer romanticize past traditions, because they are ruled by relics -- intolerant exclusivity; absolutist tendencies; patriarchy; authoritarianism; dogmatism; conservatism; transcendentalism; body-denial; sexual repression; hierarchal institutions; and all of this serves not to heighten consciousness at all, but to dissociate it.

Therefore it is to the future we look, and to those in the past who shared our forward vision -- a future where we live free, within an enlightened planetary civilization.

There is a hard road ahead. The universe is harsh and indifferent, but its laws also give us sure signs of hope and possibility. The people of Earth face some of their most daunting challenges. We will need more than just the runes, more than just magic and divination to overcome the dangers. We need the hard facts of science, and the sharp sword of skepticism. We either need our ideas to produce results, or we need to discard them and adopt better ideas.

The good news is that we have all we require to get started. We need but open our minds and embrace it.

I take comfort in knowing that the day will come when we are an ancient civilization, and I wonder what tales will still be told, what great works will provide wisdom across the abyss of time.

And to what people?

Perhaps people like ourselves.

Appendix A. Rune Alchemy.

In this book, I have made reference to the term 'alchemy' several times. Appendix A is meant to briefly detail a system of rune alchemy I have developed, and continually seek to refine. In truth, an appendix is too short to cover all aspects of the method, because I continue to discover new and powerful uses for it. Therefore in the future, a book fully dedicated to this particular system will have to be written.

If you are familiar with divination, you know that a handful of runes drawn from a bag at random can tell you an awful lot about yourself and situations you find yourself in, depending on their position. With the rune alchemy method, however, we use all 24 Elder Futhark runes, and chose their position using our current understanding of the rune meanings. We also work with them a lot longer than your typical divinatory exercise — up to a year. Because of this, you will require a journal to record the ideas, changes and results of your rune alchemy practice.

Unlike divination, this method of alchemy is far from random. It is not based on luck-of-the-draw. You will be carefully choosing the position of each rune. The positions will change as your understanding grows and your life unfolds.

You will find that you need to sit with the runes, and move them around. You may need to look up information or make notes. It is best to find some time to yourself and try to remain uninterrupted;

an hour or two on a regular basis is a good investment. Such is the cost of advancement.

The method has a number of phases, or parts. It is based around the symbol of the Valknut, an old and mysterious symbol consisting of three interlocking triangles which loosely form a larger triangle (fig. 1). In this method of rune alchemy, the Valknut represents the interwoven nature of our complex life pattern.

fig. 1 - The Valknut

The three parts of the method consist of a three-rune Persona, a nine-rune World, and the Shadow, which is composed of the leftover twelve runes in a circular outer-ring around the positions of the inner twelve.

In the first phase of the method you must figure out which three runes compose your Persona, the pattern which is essentially 'You', taken as an individual. You must identify the rune which most symbolizes 1) You, as you see yourself, 2) your innate gift, and 3) the power in life you most desire mastery over.

It may be difficult to clearly separate which is which of the three. In the beginning it may seem perhaps that there is only one rune for all three, or perhaps you have many more possibilities than a mere three. With time and contemplation, it will become known to you. Be re-assured that we have within us a relationship to every rune, and that all things are constantly in movement.

This combination symbolizes your inner-world energy — the pattern that drives your psychology. "You" are ever shifting and evolving, but in this life, an underlying pattern in the psyche has been set in motion and is discoverable. This is the psychic blueprint, the central theme, and breaks from this "real you" are only ever temporary. While it is true you can be "whatever you want to be," we often don't know what that truly is! In the rune alchemy method, you will discover that your deepest desires are also a part of you and shape your destiny, gifts and personality.

Each of the runes in the first phase form the basic triad of your inner world, your energy pattern or simply 'Persona'. (fig. 2)

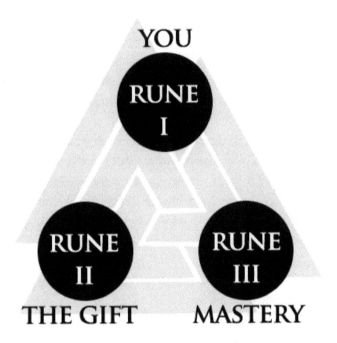

fig. 2 - Phase 1: The three-rune Persona

In the second phase, each of these three runes are the centre of yet another three runes — runes that must be discovered, whose positions must be chosen accurately (fig. 3). There is nothing random about this process. It requires great thought and observation, as well as study and active imagination on your part.

You must determine, for each of the core three runes, three runes whose meaning correlates most closely to them in your life, for a total of nine. We shall call these your 'World' runes. These can be both external-world factors, or inner-world realities. They can represent almost anything — except the 3 runes already chosen in the first phase, as your Persona, because your Persona is inextricably woven into the World.

In the second phase, we discover our relationship to our circumstances, and whatever in our world or our psyche our Persona runs up against most often. This takes keen and extensive observation of both our mind, our relationships and our environment. Our Persona runs up against visible factors in the World all the time. Each is bound to the other. For example, someone who has an incredible desire to learn but cannot afford to go to school could discover that Kenaz is part of their Persona and that Fehu was one of the three World runes linked to that aspect of their existence.

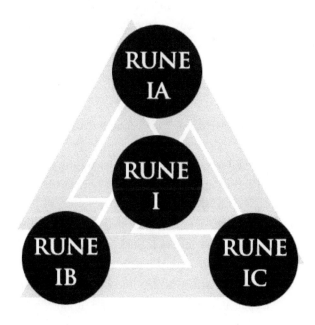

fig. 3 - Phase 2: Persona in relationship with World.

Sometimes our World runes are invisible to us. The runes you thought belonged in a certain position may change, for many reasons. The situation may change, or you may find better understanding in the form of another rune. You may outgrow a vice or correct a fault, or conquer some limitation.

We must, in this process, concern ourselves with both our ideals and our limitations. It is excellent to acknowledge both strengths and weaknesses. These are known as 'fetters'. Fetters can also be external — actual changes, abuse, social problems, economic difficulties.

After what undoubtably will be a long and slightly uncomfortable time of contemplation, you will find that you have used twelve runes. This puts You, as your 3-rune Persona within your 9-rune World.

We now enter the third phase, which is the Shadow (fig. 4). The Shadow is that which is present but not perceived in our lives — invisible or unacknowledged. This is composed of 12 runes, and we represent them in a clock-wise circle, surrounding the 3 triads already composed. For sake of simplicity, each rune will be placed and numbered according to an analogue 12-hour clock.

You will place, in order of familiarity, intrigue or recognition, each of the remaining twelve runes in a clock-wise fashion. Ideally you will study one per month over the next year — the most familiar first, to build confidence as you step into the unfamiliar, and then slowly go deeper into the unclaimed and unknown parts of ourselves and our world.

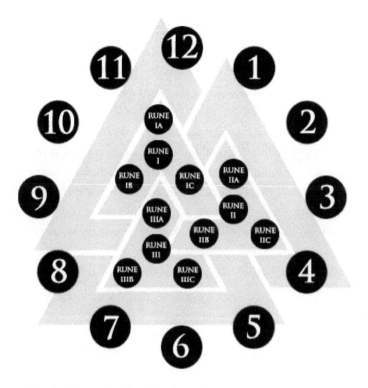

fig. 4 - Phase 3: The Shadow. Present but not perceived.

The outer circle of Shadow is the counter-point to our familiar Persona and World. It is important to understand that there are aspects of ourselves and our world that are not as they seem, or that rest, completely unobserved and unclaimed within us. These are not necessarily negative aspects, they may be quite positive ones. But until we explore them consciously, they will remain unconscious and can be troublesome giants.

At any time, you may alter the positions of these 24 runes, shifting and exchanging them one with the other so that they represent your understanding better. However, each change should be deliberate, and understood. Intuition plays a role, but this exercise is not a guessing game.

The benefit of this alchemical technique, which uses all 24 runes in a prolonged and meaningful fashion, is that while you learn the runes you meet them halfway with what you learn about yourself. It is a flexible method of discovery and transmutation, and will assist you immensely, if you are willing to think for yourself and improvise a little. You will find that rune alchemy strengthens your own special magic and brings about healing and wisdom. Hopefully it will allow you to study the runes in a way never before accessible.

Until I can write an entire book on the subject of rune alchemy, what is within these pages will have to suffice. Until then, I encourage you to participate online in the discussions — (See the end of Appendix B: Resources).

Appendix B. Resources.

I have read a lot of books and found a lot of resources over the years to drive my own thinking. But this book is composed of largely of my long contemplation and meditation on the runes themselves -- my writing here is designed to trigger *new* thought in my readers and to encourage them to activate their imagination and creativity, as I have done.

I'm not sure about the legitimacy of offering resources in that context. Sure, if I seem to agree with a community of respected authorities, I can create the appearance that I am part of those authorities. I think, though, that people may have figured out by now that I'm not too big on the notion of 'authority' when it comes to the study of the individual spirit and the deepest questions of life.

On the other hand, Rune Secrets is obviously about assisting the reader and seeker of wisdom. In this case however, I want to teach people how to actually produce results in their lives while using the runes -- something I've never been quite convinced that many rune authors are very good at, when the push comes to shove. I believe their systems may work well for themselves, but when they try to convey them, unspoken realities are lost.

So it may be better to begin to wonder what kind of resources will allow the reader to reliably construct their own rune system and achieve the results they desire from that system.

I stand apart from reference work and enter the realm of a commons -- where the community is put first rather than the guru, where the flow of wisdom is constructed as to be distributed and open-sourced, where the community benefits from the merit of a system built over time by hundreds, rather than by an individual author's personal viewpoint and hidden (or unexamined) motivations.

That's the direction I want to begin moving this. I no longer have faith in spiritual teachers, and am unwilling to join the ranks of 'respected authorities', rune teachers who believe themselves to have 'The Secret' to share, even if that belief is subtle and cloaked with a false humility. The truth is that a lot of practitioners of so called magic could afford to practice the magic of clarity and communication, as wards against the mischievous spirits of cryptic language, nonsense words and habitual mystification. I can rarely help myself from wondering if someone understands a thing they're talking about if they are unable to communicate it clearly to others. And if they are able, but unwilling? Then I question their agenda.

The irony about using the title "Rune Secrets" is that I despise secrecy. It is deeply incompatible with democracy, equality, freedom and justice. It is an attack on our search for truth, and it is with a glad heart if I am able to share something which has been, for whatever reason, kept secret from you when it comes to the runes.

No one has exclusive access to the truth. The very notion is ridiculous -- it takes the combined eyes of many to truly observe what might be. The person who is disinterested in another's viewpoint is not a wise person.

Ralph Blum, for instance, a cultural anthropologist, is often treated with condemnation by virtually every 'respected authority'. But he has single handedly done more for the rune awakening in 25 years, selling 2 MILLION copies of his plastic rune set and muddled, divination-oriented technique -- more than any so called authority. He introduces people to the runes, many of whom next go searching for specific rune meanings, or seek to expand their understanding of the runes as a whole.

What so few seem to realize is that each individual's interpretation and viewpoint regarding the runes is unique. And that interpretation and viewpoint says much more about the individual than it does about the lost mysteries of the runes themselves.

I know a better system can always be presented and more understanding can always be gained of the runes. So does anyone who picks up a copy of Blum's masterpiece. Blum made his work imperfect and incomplete on purpose -- just as, perhaps, did Odin when the tales tell of him passing the knowledge on to humankind. Odin is fond of riddles, after all. To propel people deeper into the runes, you must propel them deeper into themselves and open the world up to them. It is the genius of allowing others to become genius. When you come to understand that, you realize that Blum may indeed be a powerful rune-master. In Action. With Results. He accomplished by not accomplishing. Magic.

By not working with Blum, by stubbornly denying his, or anyone's, contribution, I fear a lot of 'respected authorities' expose themselves. To not have faith in the great many people who started with Blum and to look down dismissively on them is to reveal personal elitism. This makes sincere and curious human beings feel as if their imagination and creativity are sinful. But if you ask me, sincerity, curiosity, imagination and creativity are the most brilliant treasures, to be held onto with all of one's heart.

The ancients, our ancestors, did not have science as we know it. They did not have archaeology and anthropology like we have it today. What they had was common sense, and therefore the runes must be infused with a common wisdom. Today, I know we have a glorious academic rigor in our study of the runes and the people who used them -- but I wonder if we have as much common sense as the runes demand of us?

Common sense today will not reject the vast contributions of science when it comes to our understanding of the mind and of reality. To do so is to also reject the goals of an honest spiritual life. Who can pretend to counsel us on how our mind and spirit should be functioning in a civilization profoundly shaped by the consequences of science, if they care nothing for the demands it places upon us in the pursuit of knowledge and truth?

I know the Secret of the Runes and it is this: the runes are a living language. We use them to discuss issues that remain important to us, with one another, to sort out our thoughts, to form communities of contemplative, caring people. We use them to consciously create our lives rather than to be subject to the world's merciless indifference. The runes are very much alive -- and while I encourage a study of their history, and the archaeological evidence, I would much prefer us to recognize the runes as a living and evolving language, and to consciously develop that language for the benefit of all humankind -- regardless of race, religion or creed.

What resources can I seriously give you?

Nothing that you don't already have in your amazing human brain, trust me on that. If people had more faith in themselves (and one another) and if runic authors focused more on empowering readers, the rune community could bring ancient power and real magic into the contemporary world of today.

So the resource I will offer you is yourself.

As I write, I am building an online social network community to facilitate discussion and connection with other seekers of rune wisdom, using the Book of Rune Secrets as a starting place, not the final word. The work will grow over time as hundreds of people add to it. I will merely be an editor -- you, and others like you, will have written your own resources, because you, and others like you, will be rune masters, and it shall be I who am your humble student.

With the deepest respect,

Tyriel

Feel free to get in touch with me, and join the growing community of people seeking rune wisdom on the internet!

Email:
TYRIEL @ RUNESECRETS . COM

Blog:
RUNESECRETS . COM

Study Community:
RUNESECRETS . NET

Please be certain you sign up for the email newsletter, which will benefit you with further insight into the runes, and news about upcoming projects, such as rune music and future books, including "The Murk-Staves".

HTTP:// NEWSLETTER . RUNESECRETS . COM

To learn to use them, Seeker,
Will take you a long time,
Though helpful they are if you understand them,
Useful if you use them,
Needful if you need them.

The Wise One has spoken words in the hall,
Needful for men to know,
Unneedful for trolls to know:

Hail to the speaker,
Hail to the knower,
Joy to him who has understood,
Delight to those who have listened.

Hávamál
(The Words of Odin the High One)

www.ingramcontent.com/pod-product-compliance
Lightning Source LLC
LaVergne TN
LVHW021954200425
809137LV00011B/929

* 9 7 8 0 9 8 7 7 5 6 6 1 9 *